DATE DUE

St. Procopius College Library
Maple Ave. and College Rd.
Lisle, Illinois

TWENTIETH CENTURY INTERPRETATIONS
OF

ROBINSON
CRUSOE

A Collection of Critical Essays

Edited by

FRANK H. ELLIS

Prentice-Hall, Inc. *Englewood Cliffs, N. J.*
A SPECTRUM BOOK

Preface

During a recent week in London there might be seen at the museum in South Kensington a Victorian parlor suite in oak, the work of Thomas Tweedy (ca. 1852), of which every piece was carved with edifying scenes from *The Life and Strange Surprizing Adventures of Robinson Crusoe of York, Mariner:* Robinson Crusoe sheltered beneath a broad goatskin umbrella; Robinson Crusoe catechizing Friday; Friday baiting the bear in the tree. For sale in all the London bookshops was Muriel Spark's novel, *Robinson,* an uncanny tale of interrupted exile on an uninhabited island. And the current production at the Palladium was a pantomime in two acts entitled *Robinson Crusoe,* with Engelbert Humperdinck, the reigning star, in the title role.

As these witnesses testify, *Robinson Crusoe* has become a myth of great potency and wide application. Even in France a large umbrella is still called *un robinson.*

The purpose of the present volume is not to explore the myth, but to recall attention to the book behind the myth. Toward this end there have been assembled below a dozen critical responses to *Robinson Crusoe.* Through these insights it is hoped that the reader himself will be enabled to conjure with the power of this book.

Contents

Introduction, *by Frank H. Ellis*   1

PART ONE—*Interpretations*

Robinson Crusoe, by Virginia Woolf   19

The Author of *Robinson Crusoe, by James Sutherland*   25

Symbolic Elements in *Robinson Crusoe,*
    by Edwin B. Benjamin   34

Robinson Crusoe, Individualism and the Novel,
    by Ian Watt   39

Robinson Crusoe, by John Robert Moore   55

Defoe, *by E. M. W. Tillyard*   62

Religion and Invention in *Robinson Crusoe,*
    by William H. Halewood   79

PART TWO—*View Points*

Karl Marx: Das Kapital   90

Roger Lloyd: The Riddle of Defoe   92

Eric Berne: The Psychological Structure of Space with
    Some Remarks on *Robinson Crusoe*   94

Maximillian E. Novak: The Economic Meaning of
    Robinson Crusoe   97

George A. Starr: Robinson Crusoe and the
   Myth of Mammon   102

J. Paul Hunter: [The Un-sources of *Robinson Crusoe*]   106

Chronology of Important Dates   *111*
Notes on the Editor and Contributors   *115*
Selected Bibliography   *117*

J'avance dans *Robinson Crusoe* pas à pas,
avec l'admiration la plus vive.

ANDRÉ GIDE,
Journal 1889–1939
(Paris, 1948), p. 326

Introduction

To read in chronological order the criticism of *Robinson Crusoe* since 1900 is almost enough to restore one's faith in progress. For there can be no doubt about the progress. The evidence for it may be summarized here in one of Defoe's favorite rhetorical devices, *enumeratio,* or the list:

1. God has been discovered to be a character in *Robinson Crusoe* almost as important as he is in *Paradise Lost,* for example.

2. *Robinson Crusoe* has been discovered to be a book for adults, even for adults in the twentieth century.

3. Robinson Crusoe has been discovered to be not another name for Daniel Defoe but a fictional character created by Daniel Defoe.

4. The critics have learned not to patronize Daniel Defoe.

More may be said about each of these points, beginning with the last.

---

[1] *Defoe's Writings,* 14 vols. (Oxford: Shakespeare Head Press [1927–28]), VII, 209. In the present Introduction all references to *Robinson Crusoe,* the short title of a work which Defoe called *The Life and Strange Surprizing Adventures of Robinson Crusoe of York, Mariner,* are to this edition. *Robinson Crusoe* (1719) occupies volumes VII–VIII and its sequel, *The Farther Adventures of Robinson Crusoe* (1719), of which it was said that the publisher would have given £200 that it had never been written, occupies volumes VIII–IX.

1

1. Change in tone

The tendency to patronize Defoe began during his lifetime with remarks like Jonathan Swift's reference to "the Fellow that was *pilloryed*, I have forgot his Name." [2] The trouble of course was that Defoe was not a gentleman; his father's trade was to make and sell candles in the parish of St. Giles Cripplegate, London. Worse than that, Defoe was not a member of the Church of England as by law established. When the rector of St. Giles Cripplegate was forced out of the Church of England by the Act of Uniformity in August 1662, his parishioners James and Alice Foe followed him out of the Church of England into a Presbyterian meeting house. Something of the scorn (and perhaps even the fear) of the Church of England gentleman for the nonconformist London tradesman, which is so difficult to imagine today, is preserved in these lines from John Dryden, *The Medal* (1682):

> In Gospel phrase their Chapmen [wholesalers] they betray:
> Their Shops are Dens, the Buyer is their Prey.
> The Knack of Trades is living on the Spoyl;
> They boast, ev'n when each other they beguile.
>
> (191–94)

Defoe on the contrary boldly proclaimed that "trade in *England* makes Gentlemen" and called attention to the daughters of tradesmen married into nobility and riding through London in coaches "adorn'd with the ducal coronets." [3] Revolutionary ideas like these, of course, did not make Defoe popular with the Establishment in Church and State.

But worst of all, like William Shakespeare, Defoe was a would-be gentleman. He changed his name from plain Foe to the more impressive Defoe. He bought an expensive coach himself (which was seized in a bankruptcy suit) and paid to have a coat of arms emblazoned on the door: *Per chevron engrailed, gules and or, three griffins passant counter-changed.* But not even all this elegance could gain Defoe acceptance as a gentleman. His contemporaries were too conscious of the vulgar canting tradesman just beneath the surface. Profanity, Defoe moralized, is a breach of good manners, " 'tis imposing upon [the company] with a freedom beyond Civility; as if a Man shou'd *Fart* before a Justice." [4]

[2] *Prose Writings*, ed. Herbert Davis, 13 vols. (Oxford: Blackwell, 1939–62), II, 113.

[3] *The Complete English Tradesman* (London, 1726), pp. 374, 376.

[4] *An Essay upon Projects* (London, 1697), p. 249.

Again as in the case of Shakespeare it began to be doubted whether Defoe could have written all those works of genius that passed as his. And before the eighteenth century was over *Robinson Crusoe* had been successively attributed to Robert Harley, earl of Oxford, Dr. John Arbuthnot, the Queen's physician, and Sir Richard Steele. With the notable exceptions of Alexander Pope in the eighteenth century and Samuel Taylor Coleridge in the nineteenth century,[5] the condescending attitude toward *Robinson Crusoe* prevailed, even among his admirers, until the twentieth century. Perhaps the culmination of this tendency came in 1868 when Leslie Stephen published his essay on "Defoe's Novels" in *The Cornhill Magazine.* Sir Leslie, as he became when knighted in 1902, was a great man: he was a philosopher and historian of ideas, the first editor and chief contributor (378 articles) to *The Dictionary of National Biography,* one of the first Englishmen to ski in Switzerland, a member not of the Establishment in Church and State but of an intellectual élite, and a distinguished literary critic. Yet his attitude toward *Robinson Crusoe* may be divined from the following:

> for people who are not too proud to take a rather low order of amusement, *Robinson Crusoe* will always be one of the most charming of books.[6]

One product of this patronizing attitude is the assumption that Defoe's work is "entirely unconscious," a kind of automatic writing the effects of which were neither sought nor recognized by the author. Here again the parallel with Shakespeare, "the poet of nature," "fancies childe" warbling "his native Wood-notes wilde," is very close.[7] Leslie Stephen, for example, is quite willing to concede Defoe a large share in the discovery of the novel, but he insists that it was discovery "by a kind of accident." Stephen complains that we are "often left in doubt as to the degree in which Defoe was conscious of his own merits." He tells us that Defoe was "artistic in spite of himself" and that his effects are far from intentional.[8] Fortunately we have learned not to worry about artists' intentions. If an effect is "artistic" all we need to

[5] Pope said "The first part of *Robinson Crusoe* [is] good" (Joseph Spence, *Observations,* ed. James M. Osborn, 2 vols. [Oxford: Clarendon, 1966], I, 213; *Coleridge's Miscellaneous Criticism,* ed. Thomas M. Raysor (London: Constable, 1936), pp. 292–300.

[6] Leslie Stephen, "Defoe's novels," *The Cornhill Magazine,* XVII (January–June 1868), revised and reprinted in *Hours in a Library,* 4 vols. (New York and London: Putnam, [1907]), I, 52–53.

[7] *The Plays of William Shakespeare,* ed. Samuel Johnson, 8 vols. (London: Tonson, 1765), Preface, I, xxiv; John Milton, *L'Allegro* (1645), lines 133–34.

[8] *Hours in a Library,* I, 13, 27, 53, 60–62.

do is enjoy it and, if we are so inclined, to relate it to the context of the whole work and our own experience of similar works. We are not required to answer unanswerable questions: Did Defoe intend the artistic effect? Was he conscious of it when it was effected? Another product of this patronizing attitude is equally unfortunate. It assumes that Defoe's best effects must be borrowed. Paul Dottin, the great French scholar who adds "certainement" when there is no evidence at all, has this to say: "De Foe avait certainement, lui aussi, aperçu ce singulier personnage [Alexander Selkirk]." [9] Since he cannot believe that Defoe was capable of inventing Robinson Crusoe's experiences, M. Dottin has to believe that Alexander Selkirk, who was marooned on Juan Fernández, an uninhabited island in the Pacific, for more than four years, must have told Defoe all about it. But there are three written accounts of Selkirk's experiences and it seems likely that Defoe read them. Seals and penguins, which are strangely out of place in the tropical latitudes of Orinoco bay, both figure in the accounts of Juan Fernández, an island off the coast of Chile, open to the Antarctic. Selkirk told Woodes Rogers that he was "pester'd with Cats and Rats" and Robinson Crusoe is similarly "pester'd with Cats." [10] Selkirk also told Richard Steele that when his clothes wore out he "tacked together the Skins of Goats," [11] but details like these would be useless if Defoe himself could not imagine what it would be like to be marooned on an uninhabited island. This is the feat of imagination which the patronizing critics have refused to recognize. But Edgar Allan Poe described the situation exactly when he said, concerning *Robinson Crusoe*, "The powers which have wrought the wonder have been thrown into obscurity by the very stupendousness of the wonder they have wrought." [12] Little by little since 1900 the critics have begun to discover these powers.

2. *Robinson Crusoe is not Daniel Defoe*

The truth about Daniel Defoe that is most frequently lost sight of is that he was a poet. It was as a poet, the author of *The True-Born Englishman* (1701)—a devastating satire on the political exploitation

[9] Paul Dottin, *Daniel De Foe et ses Romans*, 3 vols. (Paris: Presses Universitaires de France, 1924), II, 301.
[10] Woodes Rogers, *A Cruising Voyage round the World* (London, 1712), p. 128; *Robinson Crusoe*, VII, 118.
[11] *The Englishman*, No. 26, December 3, 1713.
[12] *Complete Works of Edgar Allan Poe*, 10 vols. (New York: De Fau, 1902), IX, 367.

of racism—that Defoe became famous all over Europe, and he intended that another poem, *Jure Divino. A Satyr. In Twelve Books* (1706) was to have been his masterpiece. His earliest surviving work is a manuscript of 23 pages of *Meditacions* in verse, dated 1681 when Defoe was 21 years old.[13] One of his first published works is a political satire in verse entitled *A New Discovery of an Old Entreague* (1691). Thereafter he published so many satires, odes, panegyrics, and occasional verses that John Dunton supposed that he "𝕭𝖍𝖎𝖒'𝖉 in his Sleep." [14] And while it is not wholly true, as he said in July 1708, that his harp had "long since" been hung on the willows, it *is* true that after 1710 Defoe wrote almost no poetry.

Robinson Crusoe, on the contrary, seems utterly prosaic. Tropical islands in the Caribbean and the Pyrenees in winter unfold their beauties in vain before his unseeing eyes. Almost the only thing on the island to which Robinson Crusoe responds aesthetically is "a meer natural Cave," as he calls it. His description of it is indeed exciting. After crawling in for a way on all fours he is able to stand up and to light two candles:

> never was such a glorious Sight seen in the Island, I dare say, as it was to look round the Sides and Roof of this Vault, or Cave; the Walls reflected 100 thousand Lights to me from my two Candles; what was in the Rock, whether Diamonds, or any other precious Stones, or Gold, which I rather suppos'd it to be, I knew not.[15]

This is a wonderful scene, and it is pleasant to think of Daniel Defoe at home in a suburb of London imagining to himself the interior of an unexplored cave on an unnamed island in the mouth of the Orinoco River and then writing these words. But it is also a comic scene. Robinson Crusoe sees less of the beauty than of the gold, like Mammon in *Paradise Lost,*

> admiring more
> The riches of Heav'n's pavement, trodd'n Gold,
> Than aught divine or holy else enjoy'd
> In vision beatific

> (I, 681–84).

Another way in which Robinson Crusoe and Daniel Defoe differ is in their attitude toward slaves and slavery. Defoe's attitude seems to have been completely ambivalent. In one of his major poems, *Reforma-*

---

[13] *The Meditations of Daniel Defoe Now First Published,* ed. George H. Healey (Cummington, Mass.: Cummington Press, 1946).

[14] *Dunton's Whipping-Post,* 1706, p. 90.

[15] *Robinson Crusoe,* VII, 204, 207.

tion of Manners. A Satyr (1703), he strikes out bravely against the slave-traders:

> . . . harmless Natives basely they trepan,
> And barter Baubles for the *Souls of Men:*
> The Wretches they to Christian Climes bring o'er,
> To serve worse Heathens than they did before (p. 17).

But in a series of economic essays in 1709–13 Defoe defended the slave trade as potentially "the most Useful and most Profitable Trade . . . of any Part of the General Commerce of the Nation." Defoe himself paid dearly for this inconsistency, however. He bought stock in the Royal African Company, the chartered English monopoly in the slave trade, at the peak price of £400 a share and was forced to sell at less than £100—a loss, as he said, which was more than he could "bear the Weight of." What brought down the price of the stock was the large-scale intervention of unlicensed traders. Defoe wrote very feelingly about these interlopers in 1713: "the private Gain of Clandestine Trade is so sweet a Thing to some People, that . . . they care not what Injury they do to the Trade in General." [16]

But "the private Gain of Clandestine Trade" was exactly what started Robinson Crusoe on his travels. His first "Voyage to *Guinea*" yielded him a clear profit of 750 per cent and filled his mind, as he said, with "aspiring Thoughts." And it was exactly as an illegal slave trader that Robinson Crusoe began the voyage from São Salvador, Brazil, "in an evil Hour," September 1, 1659, that left him shipwrecked on the Island of Despair.[17]

A third difference between Robinson Crusoe and Daniel Defoe lies in their attitudes toward women. Sex is not even a problem for Robinson Crusoe; for him women exist only as things. On the last page of the first part of his adventures he tells us about restocking his island: "besides other Supplies," he says, "I sent seven Women." And in *The Farther Adventures of Robinson Crusoe* he adds that the oldest and ugliest of the seven "prov'd the best Wife of all the Parcel." Whether in wholesale or retail lots, women exist only as a commodity for Robinson Crusoe. Finally, when he was nearly sixty, he found it "not to [his] Disadvantage" to marry, but he tells us the names neither of his wife nor of his three children.[18]

Daniel Defoe, on the contrary, seems to have been a normally

---

[16] *Review,* VII (July 29, 1710), 212; *An Essay upon the Trade to Africa* (London, 1711), pp. 11–12; *Review,* VII (June 27, 1710), 154; *A Brief Account of the Present State of the African Trade* (London, 1713), pp. 10, 52.

[17] *Robinson Crusoe,* VII, 16, 18, 43–44, 45.

[18] *Robinson Crusoe,* VIII, 106, 190, 105.

uxorious man for whom women existed as authentic "others." He
married early, had eight children of whom six lived to maturity, and
died heartbroken at the unkindness of his son and separated from his
"dear Sophy." She was his youngest daughter whom he loved, as he
said, "More Than Ever any lovd." [19] In 1697 when he had been
married more than a dozen years Defoe published *An Essay upon
Projects,* the first work which he allowed to be published in his own
name. One of the projects which he advanced was a college for women,
a radical idea in an age when it was thought sufficient for a woman to
be able to stitch and sew and read and perhaps to write her name.
Defoe argued most eloquently that

> 'tis the sordid'st Piece of Folly and Ingratitude in the world, to with-
> hold from the Sex the due Lustre which the advantages of Education
> gives to the Natural Beauty of their Minds.
>   A Woman well Bred and well Taught, furnish'd with the additional
> Accomplishments of Knowledge and Behaviour, is *a Creature without
> comparison;* her Society is the Emblem of sublimer Enjoyments; her
> Person is Angelick, and her Conversation heavenly; she is all Softness
> and Sweetness, Peace, Love, Wit, and Delight.[20]

Once it is clearly understood that Robinson Crusoe is not simply a
"repetition" of Daniel Defoe, then it is feasible to explore—very warily
—the actual relationship between them.

Robinson Crusoe himself blurred the clear line between character
and creator when he claimed that his story was "allegorical" and insisted that "there is a Man alive, and well known too, the Actions of
whose Life are the just Subject of these Volumes, and to whom all
or most Part of the Story most directly alludes." [21] Presumably this
man is Daniel Defoe and without question there are autobiographical
fragments in *Robinson Crusoe.* Robinson Crusoe's nightmare from
which he "started up in the utmost Consternation" repeats a horrible
dream in which Defoe remembered "jumping out in a fright." [22] In
the final episode on the island Robinson Crusoe appears momentarily
"as another Person"; in April 1718, exactly a year before *Robinson
Crusoe* was published, Defoe suggested that he "might be more
Servicable in a kind of Disguise, Than if [he] appeared openly." [23]

[19] *The Letters of Daniel Defoe,* ed. George H. Healey (Oxford: Clarendon, 1955),
pp. 474, 476, 471.
[20] *An Essay upon Projects* (London, 1697), pp. 294–95.
[21] *Serious Reflections during the Life and Surprising Adventures of Robinson
Crusoe,* ed. George W. Aitken (London: J. M. Dent & Sons, Ltd., 1899), Preface, p. x.
[22] *Robinson Crusoe,* VII, 164; *Serious Reflections,* ed. Aitken, p. x.
[23] *Robinson Crusoe,* VIII, 65; *Letters of Daniel Defoe,* p. 451.

And the *"Cannibals"* whom Daniel Defoe feared were "Man-eating" loan sharks.[24]

On the other hand it must be clear that there can be no profit in trying to read *Robinson Crusoe* as a continuous allegory of the life of Daniel Defoe, in which Robinson Crusoe's rebellion against his father "represents" Defoe's refusal to be ordained a Presbyterian minister, and the like. It is unfortunate that Defoe felt it necessary to call *Robinson Crusoe* "a parable, or an allusive allegoric history," [25] but it may be possible to explain *why* he did.

Exactly what it was that Defoe thought he had written when he finished *The Life and Strange Surprizing Adventures of Robinson Crusoe* we shall never know. As James Joyce pointed out in 1912, Defoe was "The first English author to write without imitating or adapting foreign works, to create without literary models." [26] There was no existing tradition of "the novel" to which he could assimilate his new work. We do know, however, that when Charles Gildon called it "nothing but a Romance," [27] Defoe seems to have been very resentful. There were at least two reasons why Defoe could not accept *Robinson Crusoe* as a romance. In the first place, "romance" was the name of exotic, improbable prose fictions by writers like Aphra Behn, or French importations like *Hattige, or the Amours of the King of Tamaran. A Novel* (1680) by Gabriel de Brémond. Since all the effects of *Robinson Crusoe* depend upon its lifelikeness, it is easy to imagine why Defoe wished to dissociate his work from this genre.

On the other hand, "romance" also implied that what Defoe had written was not true. "Fictions and Lies" was what Charles Gildon called it, and without any tradition of realistic fiction to appeal to, Defoe was helpless. His only recourse was to insist that his work was not literally but allegorically true. "Allusive allegoric history," as he called it, when understood in the fragmentary sense suggested above, is not a bad term for the genre of *Robinson Crusoe.* For despite its title, it is not an "Adventure" in the old picaresque sense; it is not voyage literature, not a romance, not an economic fable, not a devotional tract like *The Pilgrim's Progress,* but something *new* which only later came to be called a *novel.* "And as a novelist is on the borderline between poetry and prose," Leslie Stephen said, it is here

---

[24] *An Essay on the South-Sea Trade* (London, 1712), p. 19.

[25] *Serious Reflections,* ed. Aitken, p. 101.

[26] *Daniel Defoe,* trans. by Joseph Prescott (Buffalo: State University of New York, 1964), p. 7.

[27] *The Life and Strange Surprizing Adventures of Mr. D—— De F——, of London, Hosier* (London: J. Roberts, 1719), p. 33.

that we "come . . . upon the secret of Defoe's power." [28] The prose
fictions of Defoe's old age—he was nearly sixty when he published the
first *Robinson Crusoe,* and nearly seventy when he published the
last—grow quite literally out of the poems of his earlier, buried life.

3. *A book for adults*

According to Dr. Eric Berne, "Any psychoanalyst who has not reread this remarkable work since childhood may find its depth and
interest far beyond his expectations." [29] It might be worthwhile, therefore, to ask what these depths and these interests are, not in Freudian,
but in simple literary terms.

In the most technical sense of the word, *Robinson Crusoe* is a comedy.
It is concerned with the errors and frailties of low characters. They may
be in "the upper Station of *Low Life,*" as Robinson Crusoe's father
insisted, but they are still "low" characters in the Aristotelian sense.
The plot generates a turn from misfortune to good fortune and ends
happily, as a good comedy should, in marriage. On the island some of
the humor is of the black variety: Robinson Crusoe observes that he
is likely to have few heirs; when the roof of the cave collapses, he concludes that if he had been standing under it, he would not have
needed a gravedigger. Sometimes the humor derives from simple understatement: on more than one occasion Robinson Crusoe calculates
that he "was like to have time enough to do it in," and on another he
regrets that his mustachios were not long enough to hang his hat upon,
but consoles himself with the thought that since there were "so few
to observe me . . . , it was of no manner of Consequence." [30]

The comic climax occurs when the mutineers from the English ship
wander helplessly on the island:

> We could hear them call to one another in a most lamentable Manner,
> telling one another, they were gotten into an inchanted Island; that
> either there were inhabitants in it, and they should all be murther'd,
> or else there were Devils and Spirits in it, and they should be all
> carry'd away, and devour'd.[31]

This is exactly in the style of Caliban, Stephano, and Trinculo on
another imaginary island modelled largely on the Bermudas:

[28] *Hours in a Library,* I, 29.
[29] "The psychological structure of space with some remarks on Robinson Crusoe,"
Psychoanalytic Quarterly, XXV (1956), 560; see p. 94 below.
[30] *Robinson Crusoe,* VII, 74, 85, 169, 173.
[31] *Robinson Crusoe,* VIII, 59.

Enter divers Spirits, in shape of Dogs and Hounds, hunting them about.

The parallel with *The Tempest* is so close, in fact, that John Robert Moore was able to write a plot summary which is "literally and equally true" of *The Tempest* and *Robinson Crusoe.* It ends like this:

> Most of the time the governor [Prospero-Robinson Crusoe] remains invisible, while he directs the overthrow of the enemy. These strange happenings mystify the visitors; they consider the island enchanted, and they refer to it as inhabited by devils.
> The governor restores order among the ship's company. He puts off his strange costume, dresses in European clothes, and gives up the powers which he has acquired on the island.[32]

The "ORIGINAL SIN" which led to Robinson Crusoe's punishment on the island was not a tragic flaw but a comic error. It is in fact a double error, partly religious and partly economic. Robinson Crusoe rebels against his parents' authority in order to indulge his "foolish inclination of wandring abroad." But he also indulges "a rash and immoderate Desire of rising faster than the Nature of the Thing admitted." And we all know, of course, that a rolling stone gathers no moss and that a man's reach should not exceed his grasp.[33]

But what makes *The Life and Strange Surprizing Adventures of Robinson Crusoe* a novel and not a devotional work is that our hero continues to indulge his *Wanderlust* until the end of his life. He is over 70 when, at the prospect of an overland journey from Peiping to Moscow, he says, "a secret Joy spread it self over my whole Soul, which I cannot describe, and never felt before or since." And what is even worse, this runagate amasses riches beyond the dreams of avarice. When he discovers exactly how much his fortune has increased during his 28 years on the island, he almost collapses. "It is impossible to express here," he said, "the Flutterings of my very Heart, when I . . . found all my Wealth about me. . . . In a Word, I turned pale, and grew sick; and had not the old Man run and fetch'd me a Cordial, I believe the sudden Surprize of Joy had overset Nature, and I had dy'd upon the Spot." There was no need to kill the fatted calf for this prodigal son, for he came home with "fourteen thousand sheep . . . and a thousand yoke of oxen." As Robinson Crusoe himself acknowledges—in a wry parody of *Job*—his "latter End . . . was better than the Beginning." [34]

[32] "*The Tempest* and *Robinson Crusoe,*" *Review of English Studies,* XXI (January 1945), 55–56.
[33] *Robinson Crusoe,* VII, 225, 42.
[34] *The Farther Adventures of Robinson Crusoe,* IX, 160; *Robinson Crusoe,* VIII, 81.

So the episode on the island ends, most appropriately, with a fine mock-heroic flourish. In a skirmish to regain the English ship, the rebel captain is shot through the head, "the Bullet entring at his Mouth, and came out again behind one of his Ears; so that he never spoke a Word," [35] exactly in the manner of the *Iliad:*

> Pallas Athene guided the weapon to the nose next to the eye, and it cut through the white teeth and the bronze weariless shore all the way through the tongue's base so that the spearhead came out underneath the jawbone (V, 290).

Nor does this juxtaposition seem fortuitous, for there are epic allusions throughout the island episode, such as the occasion when Robinson Crusoe imagines himself as secure as Cacus in the 8th Book of the *Aeneid:* "I fancy'd my self now like one of the ancient Giants, which are said to live in Caves, and Holes, in the Rocks, where none could come at them." [36]

This kind of juxtaposition produces effects that are ironic rather than comic. Since Robinson Crusoe was indeed likely to have few heirs so long as he remained on the island, his daydream of conveying the island "in Inheritance, as compleatly as any Lord of the Mannor in *England,*" [37] reminds us, ironically, that he had lost his own inheritance in England by running off to sea. In similar style, Robinson Crusoe's first year on the island convinced him that there was no "living Thing to fear, the biggest Creature that I had yet seen . . . being a Goat." But nearly twenty years later he is terrified by "a most monstrous frightful old He-goat . . . dying." [38] Even the old Portuguese pilot in *The Farther Adventures of Robinson Crusoe,* although his knowledge of English is as rudimentary as Friday's, learned to understand Robinson Crusoe's way of "speaking by Contraries":

> O Seignior *Inglese,* says he, you speak in Colours . . . you speak what looks white *this way,* and black *that way* . . . I understand you, Seignior *Inglese,* I understand you.[39]

As one of Defoe's contemporaries said, "He's enterprizing and BOLD," and Coleridge was of the opinion that "Defoe's irony [is] often finer than Swift's." The way of "speaking by Contraries" which Defoe adopted in *The Shortest Way with the Dissenters* (1703) was even called "the Method of *Daniel de Foe*" in 1710.[40] It is, of course, the

[35] *Robinson Crusoe,* VIII, 66.
[36] *Robinson Crusoe,* VII, 208.
[37] *Robinson Crusoe,* VII, 114.
[38] *Robinson Crusoe,* VII, 119, 206.
[39] *The Farther Adventures of Robinson Crusoe,* IX, 107, 166.
[40] John Dunton, *The Life and Errors* (London: S. Malthus, 1705), p. [246 mis-

method of *total* irony, taken up by Swift in *An Argument against Abolishing Christianity* (1711) and in *A Modest Proposal* (1729) and by Samuel Johnson in *A Compleat Vindication of the Licensers of the Stage* (1739).

It can be argued that the organizing theme of *Robinson Crusoe*, "the idea which puts the form together," is the idea of man's isolation: "man may be properly said," as Robinson Crusoe concludes, "to be alone in the midst of the crowds and hurry of men and business . . . we love, we hate, we covet, we enjoy, all in privacy and solitude." [41]

The feelings with which this idea is charged, lie, in Defoe's phrase, "between Fear and Desire": desire for at least "one Companion, one Fellow-Creature," and terror which can turn "every Stump at a Distance . . . [into] a Man." This ambivalence is polarized in two episodes which together seem to form the emotional center of the work. The fear is dramatized in Robinson Crusoe's discovery of the site of a cannibal feast and his "Horror . . . at seeing the Shore spread with Skulls, Hands, Feet, and other Bones of human Bodies." The desire is dramatized in Robinson Crusoe's discovery of the Spanish wreck and his "strange longing or hankering of Desires . . . [for] but one Soul sav'd out of this Ship." [42]

The desire-fear ambivalence is also embodied in the most frequently-recurring images in *Robinson Crusoe*. In these the problem of man's isolation is stated in the crudest possible terms: to get enough to eat and to avoid being eaten. The cannibals, Robinson Crusoe reflects, "would have seiz'd on me with the same View, as I did of a Goat." [43] Images of eating and being eaten not only predominate in *Robinson Crusoe*, they also give the work something of its literary shape.

The architectonic function of these images may be illustrated by the following examples, which are only three of the many that actually exist:

1. When Robinson Crusoe escapes from slavery in Salé (modern Rabat), he sails south along a coast where he could not go ashore without being "devour'd by savage Beasts, or more merciless Savages of human kind." Near the end of his adventures, crossing the Pyrenees in winter, Robinson Crusoe encounters a horse and two riders who

---

numbered] 240; *Passages from the Prose and Table Talk of Coleridge*, ed. W. H. Dircks (London: Walter Scott, n.d.), p. 230; *The Tale of the Cock-Match* ("The World I don't question has heard of the Trial") [1710 ?], folio half-sheet.

[41] Samuel Taylor Coleridge, "On Poesy or Art," *Biographia Literaria*, ed. J. Shawcross, 2 vols. (Oxford: Clarendon, 1907), II, 259; *Serious Reflections*, ed. Aitken, p. 2.

[42] *Robinson Crusoe*, VII, 220, 217, 178, 190.

[43] *Robinson Crusoe*, VII, 228.

had been attacked by wolves and completely "devour'd by the ravenous Creatures" (VII, 25; VIII, 99).

2. As Robinson Crusoe coasts along Mauretania he hears "hideous Howlings and Yellings" of predatory creatures on the shore. In the Pyrenees "the Howling and Yelling of those hellish Creatures," the wolves, make the nights equally horrible (VII, 26; VIII, 98).

3. Robinson Crusoe's companion in his escape from Salé, the Spanish boy, Xury, is afraid, as he says, that *"If wild mans come, they eat me."* Robinson Crusoe's man Friday is equally afraid that the cannibals will "cut him in Pieces, and eat him" (VII, 28; VIII, 18).

These details, arranged as they are in chiastic order,

devour'd	Howlings				Howling	devour'd by
by savage	and	eat me		eat him	and	ravenous
Beasts	Yellings				Yelling	Creatures
(VII, 25)	(VII, 26)	(VII, 28)		(VIII, 18)	(VIII, 98)	(VIII, 99)

provide a frame for the central action of the plot, Robinson Crusoe's confrontation with the man-eaters, which yields, as its by-product, "one Companion, one Fellow-Creature" and thus resolves the desire-fear ambivalence. This is the form, therefore, which is put together by the idea of man's isolation.

Superimposed on this form is a related pattern of dreams (isolated man talking to himself) and religious conversion (isolated man talking to God). This dream-conversion pattern is repeated on either side, so to speak, of the central confrontation—before and after, that is to say, the central episode of the plot (VII, 235–38).

Robinson Crusoe recognized that "Dreams are dangerous things to talk of,"[44] for they seem to offer equal opportunities for divine warning and for satanic suggestion. But in *Robinson Crusoe,* the conversions of Friday and of Robinson Crusoe himself are preceded and foreshadowed by dream sequences. In the case of Robinson Crusoe the dream was part of the actual process of conversion. In the literary accounts of conversion, as George W. Starr has demonstrated, four distinct stages are involved: provocation to repentance, reflection or consideration, conviction or godly sorrow, and conversion proper. The first dream clearly provided the provocation to conversion, for it was a nightmare in which an angel "in a bright Flame of Fire" lifts his spear to kill Robinson Crusoe because none of God's

[44] *Serious Reflections,* ed. Aitken, p. 250.

"afflicting Providences" have brought him to repentance.[45] In the second dream, as Robinson Crusoe recounts it, the intended victim of a cannibal feast seeks safety in Robinson Crusoe's "Fortification . . . upon which I shew'd my Ladder, made him go up." This part of the dream comes true, of course. Robinson Crusoe believed, very fatalistically, that he had been born to be his "own Destroyer," but contrari-wise, when he saw Friday fleeing from his captors, he felt "call'd plainly by Providence to save this poor Creature's Life." [46] And it is this belief which overcomes Robinson Crusoe's fear and precipitates the culminating episode of the plot, the confrontation with the man-eaters.

Friday himself, of course, is one of the man-eaters. The first thing he wants to do the morning after his escape is to dig up the dead bodies of his captors "and eat them." In the scale of nature, Robinson Crusoe locates cannibals "below even Brutality itself," so the conversion of Friday to Christianity represents a triumph of nurture over nature comparable to Robinson Crusoe's reduction of "the Woods, the Mountains, [and] the Desarts" of the island to order and usefulness.[47]

A most interesting suggestion from recent criticism of *Robinson Crusoe* is in Dewey Ganzel's argument that the episodes of Robinson Crusoe's dream of salvaging a savage, the materialization of Friday, and the conversion of Friday (VII, 225–VIII, 7), are later interpolations.[48] If this is true, these are interpolations which complete the symmetry of *Robinson Crusoe,* for they offset the dream-conversion sequence *before* the central confrontation with a dream-conversion sequence *after* the central confrontation. And when it is recalled that this pattern is enclosed in a dense framework of images of eating and being eaten, then some idea of the complexity of the structure of *Robinson Crusoe* may be gained.

It is finally a structure rich in suspense and surprise. The surprise of "the Print of a Man's naked Foot" is totally unexpected and, as Dryden said, "it is the common effect of things unexpected to surprise us into a delight." [49] An equal delight is achieved again and again with suspense. Here are some typical examples:

---

[45] George A. Starr, *Defoe and Spiritual Autobiography* (Princeton, N.J.: Princeton University Press, 1965), p. 106; *Robinson Crusoe,* VII, 100, 131.

[46] *Robinson Crusoe,* VII, 230, 235.

[47] *Robinson Crusoe,* VII, 240, 228, 130.

[48] "Chronology in *Robinson Crusoe,*" *Philological Quarterly,* XL (October 1961), 495–512.

[49] Preface to *An Evening's Love* (1671), *Essays of John Dryden,* ed. Walter P. Ker, 2 vols. (Oxford: Clarendon, 1926), I, 136.

1. After Robinson Crusoe's first discovery of cannibals, he "wore out a Year and three Months more, before [he] ever saw any more of the Savages" and then, he tells us, "I had a very strange Encounter with them." [50] Thus suspense is created for the encounter which provides the culmination of the plot. To prolong the suspense, Defoe interjects the exciting and moving episode of the Spanish wreck.

2. This pattern is repeated in "the foolish Scheme," as Robinson Crusoe calls it, of escaping from the island to the mainland with Friday. With the boat provisioned and poised for flight, Defoe interjects the exciting and bloody episode of the rescue of Friday's father and the nameless Spaniard from the cannibals.

3. When these two characters sail away in the well-provisioned piragua, Defoe interjects the totally unexpected arrival of the mutinous English ship and forces us to read *The Farther Adventures of Robinson Crusoe* if we wish to know what happened when Friday's father and the nameless Spaniard returned to the island.

James Joyce read *Robinson Crusoe* as a prophecy of empire, with Robinson Crusoe in the leading role of cool, colonizing Englishman, and he concluded that "Whoever rereads this simple, moving book in the light of subsequent history cannot help but fall under its prophetic spell." [51] But it seems no more likely that the spell of *Robinson Crusoe* depends upon its anticipations of colonial history than upon its anticipations of Freudian psychology. These are interesting accidents which serve to remind us that a work of literature is an open system—open, that is, to the effects of what happens outside it. *Robinson Crusoe* seems always ready to work its spell, but it works by such homely means as repetition, understatement, and surprise.

4. God in Robinson Crusoe

Another remarkable thing about criticism of *Robinson Crusoe* since 1900 is its handy, self-correcting feature. If Virginia Woolf complains that there is no "soul" in *Robinson Crusoe*, Mr. Halewood hurries along to show exactly when and why "soul" becomes important in *Robinson Crusoe*.[52] If M. Dottin insists that all the dates and figures

[50] *Robinson Crusoe*, VII, 214.
[51] *Daniel Defoe*, trans. by Joseph Prescott (Buffalo: State University of New York, 1964), p. 25.
[52] See pp. 21, 82 below.

are wrong, Mr. Ganzel undertakes a special study of the chronology and discovers that of the hundreds of references to time in *Robinson Crusoe*, there is "only one error." [53] If Virginia Woolf, again, complains that God does not exist in *Robinson Crusoe*, Nigel Dennis demonstrates "certainly" that "there never was a book in which God's hand was busier." [54]

It is precisely at this point that the difference between Swift and Defoe—between Establishment and dissent—becomes sharpest. The intervention of deity, whether on the stage or in the life of man, elicits from Swift a characteristic sally: "Who," he asks, "that sees a little paultry Mortal, droning, and dreaming, and drivelling to a Multitude, can think it agreeable to common good Sense, that either Heaven or Hell should be put to the Trouble of Influence or Inspection upon what he is about." Robinson Crusoe is exactly a "paultry Mortal" who discovers that "nothing can happen . . . without [God's] Knowledge or Appointment . . . And [that] if nothing happens without his Appointment, he has appointed all this to befal me." [55]

Defoe himself disclaimed "Enthusiasms, or Voices from Heaven, to Command me," but his creature, Robinson Crusoe, enjoys direct discourse with deity. So when we are told that "something" always prevented Robinson Crusoe from self-pity and that he failed to apprehend "what was really the Cause" of the earthquake, we are ready to see the hand of God working everywhere behind the scenes in *Robinson Crusoe*.[56] "Canst thou send lightning," God asks Job.

But it is not only behind the scenes that God acts in *Robinson Crusoe*. He acts as if Robinson Crusoe were his principal occupation, as M. Dottin has said. He is said to have ordered the wreck to be cast up nearer the shore so that much could be salvaged. Besides many "unknown Deliverances," he delivers Robinson Crusoe from being carried out to sea in his boat, he delivers him from slaughtering the cannibals, and, of course, from being slaughtered by them. God calls upon Robinson Crusoe to save Friday, awakens two of the mutineers to save their lives, but ensnares the leaders of the mutiny "in their own Ways." This is what Charles Gildon meant by the "Coining of Providences" in *Robinson Crusoe*.[57]

[53] *Daniel De Foe et ses Romans*, 3 vols. (Paris: Presses Universitaires de France, 1924), II, 502–3; *Philological Quarterly*, XL (October 1961), 496.

[54] See p. 22 below; *Jonathan Swift. A Short Character* (New York: The Macmillan Company, 1964), p. 125.

[55] *A Discourse concerning the Mechanical Operation of the Spirit* (1704), *Prose Writings*, ed. Herbert Davis, I, 180; *Robinson Crusoe*, VII, 106.

[56] *Review*, II (October 13, 1705), 381; *Robinson Crusoe*, VII, 156–57, 71, 91.

[57] *Robinson Crusoe*, VII, 150, 228, 163, 200, 202–3, 235; VIII, 48, 70; *The Life and*

Twenty-five years of solitary confinement is God's punishment of Robinson Crusoe. Robinson Crusoe speaks of the island again and again as a prison and of his life on the island as "this Death of a Life." [58] Ian Watt, among others, complains of the unreality of Robinson Crusoe's behavior on the island and cites historical examples of marooned seamen who went mad. But Robinson Crusoe's behavior cannot appear totally unrealistic for V. S. Pritchett has said that "An Englishman on a desert island *would*, in all probability, behave as Crusoe did." [59]

Surely the point must be that Robinson Crusoe's behavior on the island reenacts a drama of religious conversion, not a controlled experiment in the effects of solitary confinement. It is, in fact, almost a dramatization of Pascal's celebrated wager: Robinson Crusoe loses twenty-five years of sinful life, but he gains an eternity of bliss. At the moment of his conversion, "in a Kind of Extasy of Joy," as he recalls, "I cry'd out aloud, *Jesus, thou Son of David, Jesus thou exalted Prince and Saviour, give me Repentance!*" [60] Robinson Crusoe's "captivity" was primarily theological and only incidentally geographical. Or to put it another way: Robinson Crusoe's solitary confinement to the island is the vehicle of a metaphor of which the tenor is his captivity in sin.

As Martin J. Greif puts it, Robinson Crusoe "is enabled through the gift of divine grace to contribute to his own physical survival on the island." [61] Robinson Crusoe himself knows how he would have lived on the island without the salvage which God provided: if he had got nothing out of the ship, he says, he could have survived only as an animal, tearing raw flesh "with my Claws like a Beast." [62]

Before Robinson Crusoe's conversion, the island is *"the Island of Despair,"* but his "Extasy of Joy" at the moment of conversion is extrapolated in new explorations. Moving inland, Robinson Crusoe discovers a hidden valley, a "delicious Vale" with

Mellons upon the Ground in great Abundance . . . and the Clusters of Grapes were just now in their Prime, very ripe and rich . . . the Country appear'd so fresh, so green, so flourishing, every thing being in

Strange Surprizing Adventures of Mr. D—— De F——, of London, Hosier (London: J. Roberts, 1719), p. 8.

[58] *Robinson Crusoe*, VII, 111, 130, 231.

[59] See pp. 50–51 below; V. S. Pritchett, "Defoe," *The English Novelists*, ed. Derek Verschoyle (New York: Harcourt, Brace & World, Inc., 1936), p. 66.

[60] *Robinson Crusoe*, VII, 110.

[61] "The conversion of Crusoe," *Studies in English Literature*, VI (Summer 1966), 553.

[62] *Robinson Crusoe*, VII, 150–51.

a constant Verdure, or Flourish of *Spring*, that it looked like a planted Garden . . . I saw here Abundance of Cocoa Trees, Orange, and Lemon, and Citron Trees, but all wild.[63]

Seen for a moment through the eyes of a recent convert, *"the Island of Despair"* looks like a *paradis terrestre.* This in turn reminds us again that the island was modelled partly on the Bermudas where God provided sanctuary for other nonconformists:

> He gave us this eternal Spring,
> Which here enamells every thing; . . .
> He hangs in shades the Orange bright,
> Like golden Lamps in a green Night. . . .
> He makes the Figs our mouths to meet;
> And throws the Melons at our feet.[64]

Robinson Crusoe's island is not in the Bermudas, of course, but in the mouth of the Orinoco and as he wrote Defoe had before him charts of the river and its shores. South of the river lay the Guianas, still largely unexplored, an area in which Defoe had been interested for thirty years.

Defoe thought of himself as "originally a Projector" and one of his favorite projects was to colonize the Guianas, which he believed to be rich in gold. Shortly after *Robinson Crusoe,* Defoe published *An Historical Account of the Voyages and Adventures of Sir Walter Raleigh. With the Discoveries and Conquests He made for the Crown of England. Also a Particular Account of His Several Attempts for the Discovery of the Gold Mines in Guiana* (1719). In this work he pointed out to the South Sea Company, which monopolized English trade in the Caribbean, that their charter began at the river Orinoco and that he was "ready to lay before them a Plan or Chart of the Rivers and Shores, the Depths of Water, and all necessary Instructions for the Navigation, with a Scheme of the Undertaking, which he had the Honour about thirty Years ago, to lay before King *William,* and to demonstrate how easy it would be to bring the attempt to Perfection." [65] The gold mines in Guiana were soon worked out, but the by-product, *The Life and Strange Surprizing Adventures of Robinson Crusoe,* proved to be infinitely more rewarding.

[63] *Robinson Crusoe*, VII, 79, 113–15.

[64] Andrew Marvell, *Bermudas* (1681), lines 13–22.

[65] *The Political History of the Devil* (London, 1726), p. 298; *An Historical Account of the Voyages and Adventures of Sir Walter Raleigh* (London: W. Boreham, 1719), p. 55.

PART ONE

Interpretations

Robinson Crusoe

by Virginia Woolf

There are many ways of approaching this classical volume; but which shall we choose? Shall we begin by saying that, since Sidney died at Zutphen leaving the *Arcadia* unfinished, great changes had come over English life, and the novel had chosen, or had been forced to choose, its direction? A middle class had come into existence, able to read and anxious to read not only about the loves of princes and princesses, but about themselves and the details of their humdrum lives. Stretched upon a thousand pens, prose had accommodated itself to the demand; it had fitted itself to express the facts of life rather than the poetry. That is certainly one way of approaching *Robinson Crusoe*—through the development of the novel; but another immediately suggests itself—through the life of the author. Here too, in the heavenly pastures of biography, we may spend many more hours than are needed to read the book itself from cover to cover. The date of Defoe's birth, to begin with, is doubtful—was it 1660 or 1661? Then again, did he spell his name in one word or in two? And who were his ancestors? He is said to have been a hosier; but what, after all, was a hosier in the seventeenth century? He became a pamphleteer, and enjoyed the confidence of William the Third; one of his pamphlets caused him to be stood in the pillory and imprisoned at Newgate; he was employed by Harley and later by Godolphin; he was the first of the hireling journalists; he wrote innumerable pamphlets and articles; also *Moll Flanders* and *Robinson Crusoe*; he had a wife and six children; was spare in figure, with a hooked nose, a sharp chin, grey eyes and a large mole near his mouth. Nobody who has any slight acquaintance with English literature needs to be told how many hours can be spent and how many lives have

Virginia Woolf, "Robinson Crusoe," The Second Common Reader (New York: Harcourt, Brace & World, Inc. [1932?]), pp. 50–58. Copyright 1932 by Leonard Woolf. Reprinted by permission of Harcourt, Brace & World, Inc. and Leonard Woolf.

been spent in tracing the development of the novel and in examining the chins of the novelists. Only now and then, as we turn from theory to biography and from biography to theory, a doubt insinuates itself— if we knew the very moment of Defoe's birth and whom he loved and why, if we had by heart the history of the origin, rise, growth, decline, and fall of the English novel from its conception (say) in Egypt to its decease in the wilds (perhaps) of Paraguay, should we suck an ounce of additional pleasure from *Robinson Crusoe* or read it one whit more intelligently?

For the book itself remains. However we may wind and wriggle, loiter and dally in our approach to books, a lonely battle waits us at the end. There is a piece of business to be transacted between writer and reader before any further dealings are possible, and to be reminded in the middle of this private interview that Defoe sold stockings, had brown hair, and was stood in the pillory is a distraction and a worry. Our first task, and it is often formidable enough, is to master his perspective. Until we know how the novelist orders his world, the ornaments of that world, which the critics press upon us, the adventures of the writer, to which biographers draw attention, are superfluous possessions of which we can make no use. All alone we must climb upon the novelist's shoulders and gaze through his eyes until we, too, understand in what order he ranges the large common objects upon which novelists are fated to gaze: man and men; behind them Nature; and above them that power which for convenience and brevity we may call God. And at once confusion, misjudgment, and difficulty begin. Simple as they appear to us, these objects can be made monstrous and indeed unrecognisable by the manner in which the novelist relates them to each other. It would seem to be true that people who live cheek by jowl and breathe the same air vary enormously in their sense of proportion; to one the human being is vast, the tree minute; to the other, trees are huge and human beings insignificant little objects in the background. So, in spite of the textbooks, writers may live at the same time and yet see nothing the same size. Here is Scott, for example, with his mountains looming huge and his men therefore drawn to scale; Jane Austen picking out the roses on her tea-cups to match the wit of her dialogues; while Peacock bends over heaven and earth one fantastic distorting mirror in which a tea-cup may be Vesuvius or Vesuvius a tea-cup. Nevertheless Scott, Jane Austen, and Peacock lived through the same years; they saw the same world; they are covered in the text-books by the same stretch of literary history. It is in their perspective that they are different. If, then, it were granted us to grasp this firmly, for ourselves, the battle would end in victory; and we could turn, secure in our intimacy, to enjoy the various delights with which the critics and biographers so generously supply us.

But here many difficulties arise. For we have our own vision of the world; we have made it from our own experience and prejudices, and it is therefore bound up with our own vanities and loves. It is impossible not to feel injured and insulted if tricks are played and our private harmony is upset. Thus when *Jude the Obscure* appears or a new volume of Proust, the newspapers are flooded with protests. Major Gibbs of Cheltenham would put a bullet through his head tomorrow if life were as Hardy paints it; Miss Wiggs of Hampstead must protest that though Proust's art is wonderful, the real world, she thanks God, has nothing in common with the distortions of a perverted Frenchman. Both the gentleman and the lady are trying to control the novelist's perspective so that it shall resemble and reinforce their own. But the great writer—the Hardy or the Proust—goes on his way regardless of the rights of private property; by the sweat of his brow he brings order from chaos; he plants his tree there, and his man here; he makes the figure of his deity remote or present as he wills. In masterpieces—books, that is, where the vision is clear and order has been achieved—he inflicts his own perspective upon us so severely that as often as not we suffer agonies—our vanity is injured because our own order is upset; we are afraid because the old supports are being wrenched from us; and we are bored—for what pleasure or amusement can be plucked from a brand new idea? Yet from anger, fear, and boredom a rare and lasting delight is sometimes born.

Robinson Crusoe, it may be, is a case in point. It is a masterpiece, and it is a masterpiece largely because Defoe has throughout kept consistently to his own sense of perspective. For this reason he thwarts us and flouts us at every turn. Let us look at the theme largely and loosely, comparing it with our preconceptions. It is, we know, the story of a man who is thrown, after many perils and adventures, alone upon a desert island. The mere suggestion—peril and solitude and a desert island—is enough to rouse in us the expectation of some far land on the limits of the world; of the sun rising and the sun setting; of man, isolated from his kind, brooding alone upon the nature of society and the strange ways of men. Before we open the book we have perhaps vaguely sketched out the kind of pleasure we expect it to give us. We read; and we are rudely contradicted on every page. There are no sunsets and no sunrises; there is no solitude and no soul. There is, on the contrary, staring us full in the face nothing but a large earthenware pot. We are told, that is to say, that it was the 1st of September 1651; that the hero's name is Robinson Crusoe; and that his father has the gout. Obviously, then, we must alter our attitude. Reality, fact, substance is going to dominate all that follows. We must hastily alter our proportions throughout; Nature must furl her splendid purples; she is only the giver of drought and water; man must be reduced to a struggling, life-preserving animal; and God shrivel into a magistrate whose seat, substantial and somewhat hard, is only a little way above the horizon. Each sortie of ours in pursuit of information upon these cardinal points of perspective—God, man, Nature—is snubbed back with ruthless commonsense. Robinson Crusoe thinks of God: "sometimes I would expostulate with myself, why providence should thus completely ruin its creatures. . . . But something always return'd swift upon me to check these thoughts." God does not exist. He thinks of Nature, the fields "adorn'd with flowers and grass, and full of very fine woods," but the important thing about a wood is that it harbours an abundance of parrots who may be tamed and taught to speak. Nature does not exist. He considers the dead, whom he has killed himself. It is of the utmost importance that they should be buried at once, for "they lay open to the sun and would presently be offensive." Death does not exist. Nothing exists except an earthenware pot. Finally, that is to say, we are forced to drop our own preconceptions and to accept what Defoe himself wishes to give us.

Let us then go back to the beginning and repeat again, "I was born in the year 1632 in the city of York of a good family." Nothing could be plainer, more matter of fact, than that beginning. We are drawn on soberly to consider all the blessings of orderly, industrious middle-class life. There is no greater good fortune we are assured than to be born of the British middle class. The great are to be pitied and so are the poor; both are exposed to distempers and uneasiness; the middle station between the mean and the great is the best; and its virtues—temperance, moderation, quietness, and health—are the most desirable. It was a sorry thing, then, when by some evil fate a middle class youth was bitten with the foolish love of adventure. So he proses on, drawing, little by little, his own portrait, so that we never forget it—imprinting upon us indelibly, for he never forgets it either, his shrewdness, his caution, his love of order and comfort and respectability; until by whatever means, we find ourselves at sea, in a storm; and, peering out, everything is seen precisely as it appears to Robinson Crusoe. The waves, the seamen, the sky, the ship—all are seen through those shrewd, middle-class, unimaginative eyes. There is no escaping him. Everything appears as it would appear to that naturally cautious, apprehensive, conventional, and solidly matter-of-fact intelligence. He is incapable of enthusiasm. He has a natural slight distaste for the sublimities of Nature. He suspects even Providence of exaggeration. He is so busy and has such an eye to the main chance that he notices only a tenth part of what is going on round him. Everything is capable of a rational explanation, he is sure, if only he had time to attend to it. We are much more alarmed by the "vast great creatures" that swim out in the night and surround his boat than he is. He at once takes his gun and fires at them, and off they swim—whether they are lions or not he really cannot say. Thus before we know it we are opening our mouths wider and wider. We are swallowing monsters that we should have jibbed at if they had been offered us by an imaginative and flamboyant traveller. But anything that this sturdy middle-class man notices can be taken for a fact. He is for ever counting his barrels, and making sensible provisions for his water supply; nor do we ever find him tripping even in a matter of detail. Has he forgotten, we wonder, that he has a great lump of beeswax on board? Not at all. But as he had already made candles out of it, it is not nearly as great on page thirty-eight as it was on page twenty-three. When for a wonder he leaves some inconsistency hanging loose—why if the wild cats are so very tame are the goats so very shy?—we are not seriously perturbed, for we are sure that there was a reason, and a very good one, had he time to give it us. But the pressure of life when one is fending entirely for oneself alone on a desert island is really no laughing matter. It is no crying one either. A man must have an eye to everything; it is no time for raptures about Nature when the lightning may explode one's gunpowder—it is imperative to seek a safer lodging for it. And so by means of telling the truth undeviatingly as it appears to him— by being a great artist and forgoing this and daring that in order to give effect to his prime quality, a sense of reality—he comes in the end to make common actions dignified and common objects beautiful. To dig, to bake, to plant, to build—how serious these simple occupations are; hatchets, scissors, logs, axes—how beautiful these simple objects become. Unimpeded by comment, the story marches on with magnificent downright simplicity. Yet how could comment have made it more impressive? It is true that he takes the opposite way from the psychologist's—he describes the effect of emotion on the body, not on the mind. But when he says how, in a moment of anguish, he clinched his hands so that any soft thing would have been crushed; how "my teeth in my head would strike together, and set against one another so strong, that for the time I could not part them again," the effect is as deep as pages of analysis could have made it. His own instinct in the matter is right. "Let the naturalists," he says, "explain these things, and the reason and manner of them; all

I can say to them is, to describe the fact. . . ." If you are Defoe, certainly to describe the fact is enough; for the fact is the right fact. By means of this genius for fact Defoe achieves effects that are beyond any but the great masters of descriptive prose. He has only to say a word or two about "the grey of the morning" to paint vividly a windy dawn. A sense of desolation and of the deaths of many men is conveyed by remarking in the most prosaic way in the world, "I never saw them afterwards, or any sign of them except three of their hats, one cap, and two shoes that were not fellows." When at last he exclaims, "Then to see how like a king I din'd too all alone, attended by my servants"—his parrot and his dog and his two cats, we cannot help but feel that all humanity is on a desert island alone—though Defoe at once informs us, for he has a way of snubbing off our enthusiasms, that the cats were not the same cats that had come in the ship. Both of those were dead; these cats were new cats, and as a matter of fact cats became very troublesome before long from their fecundity, whereas dogs, oddly enough, did not breed at all.

Thus Defoe, by reiterating that nothing but a plain earthenware pot stands in the foreground, persuades us to see remote islands and the solitudes of the human soul. By believing fixedly in the solidity of the pot and its earthiness, he has subdued every other element to his design; he has roped the whole universe into harmony. And is there any reason, we ask as we shut the book, why the perspective that a plain earthenware pot exacts should not satisfy us as completely, once we grasp it, as man himself in all his sublimity standing against a background of broken mountains and tumbling oceans with stars flaming in the sky?

The Author of *Robinson Crusoe*

by James Sutherland

By this time [1719] Defoe was close upon sixty. Had he died now he would not have been quite forgotten, but it is unlikely that any one would have considered it worth while to write his biography. Hitherto, he had given up to party what (as he was soon to prove) was meant for mankind; and party writings rarely survive the occasion that gave rise to them, except for the historian, who alone takes the trouble to find out what they were about. But now, at the age of fifty-nine, Defoe did something for mankind. And having once begun, he continued for five astonishing years to work with varying success the new vein that he had discovered in himself. What he did was *Robinson Crusoe*; or rather,

> The Life and Strange Surprizing Adventures of *Robinson Crusoe,* of York, Mariner: Who lived Eight and Twenty Years, all alone in an un-inhabited Island on the Coast of America, near the Mouth of the Great River of Oroonoque; Having been cast on Shore by Shipwreck, wherein all the Men perished but himself. With an Account how he was at last strangely deliver'd by Pyrates. *Written by Himself.*

Having tried his hand at verse satire and prose satire, at political and religious controversy, at history, at journalism, at the essay, at the ode and the hymn and the panegyric, at straightforward narrative and semi-fictitious narrative, he was now in his declining years turning his attention to prose fiction. If one can judge of such things in terms of social values, he was undoubtedly coming down in the world when he wrote *Robinson Crusoe.* For an author who had engaged with success in political and religious controversy to turn his hand to tales of adventure, was—to the eighteenth-century way of thinking—a sign of social, if not indeed of intellectual, decay. Let there be no mistake about it: the class to which Defoe addressed his *Robinson Crusoe* was the class that read *Mist's Journal*—the small shopkeepers and artisans,

From James Sutherland, Defoe *(Philadelphia and New York: J. B. Lippincott Co., 1938), pp. 227–46. Reprinted by permission of J. B. Lippincott Co. and Methuen & Company Ltd.*

the publicans, the footmen and servant wenches, the soldiers and sailors, those who could read but who had neither the time nor the inclination to read very much. "There is not an old woman," wrote one of his sneering critics, "that can go to the price of it, but buys thy *Life and Adventures,* and leaves it, as a legacy, with the *Pilgrim's Progress,* the *Practice of Piety,* and *God's Revenge against Murther* to her posterity." Others read the book too, but it was not intended for the lady and the gentleman.[1]

And this, of course, is true of all the fictitious narratives that succeeded it. Defoe was reaching a new public; it might even be said that he was creating one. The contempt with which writers like Pope allude to Defoe is instructive; they sneer because they are secretly uneasy. Here was this fellow, throwing off book after book, and he had no business to be writing at all. He was outside the "ring"; he had not graduated from the recognized school of authorship. His Latin was contemptible, he paid far too little attention to polite diction—he actually wrote more or less as he spoke—and he was full of vulgar sentiments that appealed to the lower orders. And yet Pope *felt* that he was a remarkable writer. "The first part of *Robinson Crusoe* is very good," he admitted privately. "De Foe wrote a vast many things; and none bad, though none excellent, except this. There is something good in all he has written."

There was never any doubt about the popularity of *Robinson Crusoe.* It appeared in April 1719, and it was to keep the printers busy for a long time to come. No one thought of taking Defoe's story seriously as literature; the gentleman and the scholar affected to despise it, the book-collector and the university professor were not to appear until much later. But if Defoe's public was drawn chiefly from the middle and the lower classes, that public had got an epic entirely after its own heart, with a hero it could understand and admire because he was taken from its own ranks. Crusoe may be all Mankind in difficulties, but he is first of all an Englishman of the lower middle classes making the best of things. It is his isolation that gives him his hold upon the imagination, but it is his homely virtues and his refusal to become heroic that keep him human, and human in an English way. Defoe never allows Crusoe to become a tragic figure; he is the ordinary decent man triumphing over circumstances, and making such a remarkable job of it that we are sorry in the end that he has to be rescued and sent back to a world of ease and plenty.

Defoe, in fact, has handled the situation with remarkable care and

[1] *The Life and Strange Surprizing Adventures of Mr. D—— De F—— of London, Hosier,* C. Gildon. (Quoted in *Lee,* p. 298.)

skill for one who wrote so rapidly and carelessly. He has thought things out. He has realized, for instance, that we are not going to be nearly so interested in Crusoe if he simply lives like a wild man on nuts and grapes and goat's milk. A certain Henry Pitman, from whose adventures Defoe probably took a few hints, had been reduced, when in similar circumstances to Crusoe, to smoking a sort of "wild sage"; and, having no pipe, he smoked it in a cat's claw. Such facts have a certain macabre appeal, and Defoe's hero has occasionally to content himself with such inadequate makeshifts. But a great part of the charm of Crusoe's story lies in the fact that he ends up, after beginning with only a few things saved from the wreck, by having most of the comforts of civilization, or at any rate a good imitation of them. A less skilled writer would have set him on the island with only a jack-knife: Defoe allows him to retrieve a considerable number of useful articles—two saws, an axe, a hammer, the whole of the carpenter's chest, two very good fowling pieces and two pistols, some powder horns and a bag of small shot, three barrels of gunpowder (one damp), two old rusty swords, two or three bags full of nails and spikes, and, above all, "that most useful thing called a grindstone." It is a beginning, at any rate, and with those small aids he proceeds to build up a new life. To read *Robinson Crusoe* is to be compelled to face up to all sorts of physical problems that civilized man has long since forgotten. It is in some sense to retrace the history of the human race; it is certainly to look again with the unspoilt eyes of childhood on many things that one had long since ceased to notice at all.[2]

If ever there was a self-made man it is Robinson Crusoe; he is the sober industrious Englishman, hardened by difficulties but not overwhelmed by them, making his mistakes and then trying again, enjoying his own ingenuity and properly resigned to his lot. Defoe was too well-travelled a man to believe that his countrymen must of necessity prove superior on every occasion to those who had not the felicity to be true-born Englishmen. But he did believe that an honest Englishman was hard to beat. One of the Spaniards rescued by Crusoe puts the case for the Englishman admirably. "He told me," says Crusoe,

> it was remarkable that Englishmen had a greater presence of mind in their distress than any people that ever he met with; that their unhappy nation and the Portuguese were the worst men in the world to struggle with misfortunes; for that their first step in dangers, after

[2] J. Spence, *Anecdotes; A Relation of the Great Sufferings . . . of Henry Pitman,* 1689. (*An English Garner,* vol. VII, p. 362).

the common efforts are over, was always to despair, lie down under it, and die, without rousing their thoughts up to proper remedies for escape.

Like a good Englishman, Crusoe insists that he has really done very little, and that anybody in his circumstances would have acted in much the same way. But the Spaniard knows better,

> "Seignor," says the Spaniard, "had we poor Spaniards been in your case, we should never have gotten half those things out of the ship, as you did. Nay," says he, "we should never have found means to have gotten a raft to carry them, or to have gotten the raft on shore without boat or sail; and how much less should we have done it," said he, "if any of us had been alone!" [3]

It is characteristic, too, of this shipwrecked Englishman that through all his misfortunes he keeps his self-respect. There is no need, Defoe feels, for Crusoe to neglect his clothes and walk about like a naked savage, and he sees to it that his hero remains decently covered. Not that it would have mattered very much, for with all its morality there is a strange innocence about Defoe's story; its emotions are real enough, and yet its actions are oddly removed from the moral world. Stealing on Crusoe's island is impossible, but the satisfactory emotions of successful theft are at least suggested by his looting of the wreck. There can be no cheating of one's fellows upon an island inhabited by one man; but that emotion, too, is gratified to some extent by Crusoe's getting the better of nature, his outwitting of the birds that are eating his corn, his taming of the goats, and all the little stratagems by which he overcame the hostility of natural forces. Yet as far as morality can be said to exist in such circumstances, Crusoe is a thoroughly moral man; and later, becoming religious, he takes to reading his Bible, but in a manly sort of way. There is nothing very fine or subtle about Crusoe; he is simply, like his creator, a practical, level-headed, intelligent, and resolute Englishman who has inherited the sterling qualities of the middle class into which he was born. He is, indeed, Daniel Defoe as he might have been but for the grace of God.

Some months later Defoe actually suggested in his *Serious Reflections during the Life of Robinson Crusoe* that Crusoe's story was an allegory of his own life. It would be unwise to take this statement very seriously. Defoe was fond of parading the pageant of his misfortunes before an unsympathetic public; and it may have occurred to him after he had finished *Robinson Crusoe*—or even while he was still writing it—that his hero's misadventures had in some respects an allegorical resem-

---

[3] *Robinson Crusoe* (Bohn's Illustrated Library, 1855), p. 307.

blance to those of his own life.[4] But to identify Crusoe's shipwreck with Defoe's bankruptcy, to look for a man Friday among his acquaintances, and to search everywhere for parallels between the career of the real Defoe and the imaginary Crusoe, can lead only to fantastic speculations.[5] As a Puritan Defoe seems always to have felt compelled to apologize for writing "mere fictions." His favourite defence was, of course, that his stories conveyed a moral lesson; and if he could persuade the public to believe that *Robinson Crusoe* was a sort of moral allegory he would lose no readers who were looking for a good story and might gain several who wanted only a good moral.

For the great and continuing success of *Robinson Crusoe* there are several good reasons. Defoe's later stories show plenty of narrative skill and inventiveness. Some of them have more than one interesting character to attract the reader, and all of them contain striking examples of his realistic methods. Yet those other narratives are hardly known outside England, and in England they are not much read outside the universities. Undoubtedly the appeal of *Robinson Crusoe* lies to a great extent in the hero's situation. What has attracted readers at all times is that part of Crusoe's life when he is alone, or alone with Friday, on his desert island. The later adventures are exciting enough, but no more memorable than the adventures of Captain Singleton, and considerably less interesting to most adult readers than those of Moll Flanders or Roxana. But though a picturesque situation will account for much of the delight that readers have always taken in *Robinson Crusoe*—and in *Gulliver's Travels*—it will not explain everything.

The fact is that in his story of a shipwrecked mariner Defoe has succeeded in touching some of the most powerful chords in the human heart. There is, for instance, the human delight in making things—strongest in the child or the artist, but present in varying degrees in the minds of most normal adults. Crusoe was badly in need of some earthenware vessels for storing his food, and before long he set about trying to "botch up" some sort of pot.

> It would make the reader pity me, or rather laugh at me, to tell how many awkward ways I took to raise this paste; what odd, misshapen, ugly things I made; how many of them fell in, and how many fell out, the clay not being stiff enough to bear its own weight; how many cracked by the over violent heat of the sun, being set out too hastily;

[4] The suggestion seems to have come to him from Charles Gildon, who in September 1719 attacked him in a pamphlet called *The Life and Strange Surprizing Adventures of Mr. D. . . . De F. . . . of London, Hosier. . . .*

[5] There would be more justification for identifying Crusoe with Robert Harley, and the faithful Friday with Defoe.

and how many fell in pieces with only removing, as well before as after they were dried; and, in a word, how, after having laboured hard to find the clay—to dig it, to temper it, to bring it home, and work it— I could not make above two large earthen ugly things (I cannot call them jars) in about two months' labour.

No doubt the reader pities Crusoe, and perhaps he laughs at him a little too; but above all he shares in his efforts to create. At last Crusoe stumbles upon the secret of the pot-making: it is no good trying to bake them in the heat of the sun—they must be burnt on a fire.

> This set me to studying how to order my fire, so as to make it burn some pots. I had no notion of a kiln, such as the potters burn in, or of glazing them with lead, tho' I had some lead to do it with; but I placed three large pipkins and two or three pots in a pile one upon another, and placed my fire-wood all round it, with a great heap of embers under them. I plied the fire with fresh fuel round the outside, and upon the top, till I saw the pots in the inside red-hot quite through, and observed that they did not crack at all. . . .[6]

All night Crusoe sat by the fire watching his pots glowing among the red-hot embers, until the heat gradually abated. And in the morning, there they were—"three very good (I will not say handsome) pipkins and two other earthen pots, as hard burnt as could be desired, and one of them perfectly glazed with the running of the sand." So, too, he makes himself an umbrella, and a goatskin cap, and breeches "made of the skin of an old he-goat," and, after a disastrous error of judgement, a little boat to sail in.

The reader experiences another sort of delight in watching how Crusoe succeeds in "making things do." He is full of that ingenuity which finds expression in all sorts of extraordinary devices to mend things that are broken or replace things that are lost. When Crusoe had managed to raise a little field of corn (having first dug the ground with a wooden spade of his own making, and harrowed it by dragging a heavy branch across it), he was faced with the problem of how to cut it without a scythe. So he made one. He made it, as well as he could, out of one of the cutlasses which he had saved from the wreck.

There is, too, the delight of unexpectedly discovering things— whether it is a bag of nails, or a valley full of grapes and melons. There is Crusoe's proprietary pride in watching the seeds that he has sown sending up green blades through the soil, and in contemplating how his goats and his cats have multiplied their species. There is his whole world of make-believe—the little fortification that he calls his castle, the three loaded musquets that he thinks of as his cannon,

[6] *Ibid.*, pp. 93–94.

and his country seat with its bowers and enclosures. Crusoe, in fact, is playing at "houses," and most of his readers can sympathize with his pretence. . . .

Defoe knew all about ships, too. He had bought and sold them, and his brother-in-law, Francis Bartham, was a shipbuilder. Even in some of the incidents in *Robinson Crusoe* one can see Defoe turning some of his more particular knowledge to account. When Crusoe describes how he made his clay pots there is no danger of Defoe falling into any mistake, for if he had run a brick-and-tile factory for several years he ought to have known all about the baking of clay. . . .[7]

It is clear, therefore, that the author of fifty-nine who suddenly began giving the world a series of fictitious narratives was still to a considerable extent upon the familiar ground of fact. Nor was he unprepared for the change in technique which this new form of writing demanded. His long career as a journalist had taught him how to present his facts in an easy narrative style; and such lively and realistic reporting as he had achieved in the *Apparition of Mrs. Veal* was an excellent preparation for the imaginative reporting of *Robinson Crusoe*.[8] Almost all his narratives, too, are told in the first person: many years of dramatizing himself in the *Review* had made this form of expression second nature to Defoe. The *Review* had other fictitious elements, notably dialogue. Defoe frequently enlivened his argument with a bit of racy conversation:

> Let any English gentleman but reflect as he walks along the *Strand,* with his footmen behind him, as he goes by the Mercer's or Draper's shops etc. "Jack," says one to t'other; "here's Sir John——a-coming." As he goes by 'tis a low bow, and all obeisance in the world; when he is gone, "Ay, d—m him, he has got my coat upon his back, he'll wear it out before I shall be paid for it." "Ay, and that's my master's periwig he has on too," says the Barber's boy. "I wou'd he would send it to-morrow to be put in the buckle; I'm sure my master wou'dn't let him have it again till he was paid for it."—"Who, Sir John——?" says the Milliner. "He owes my master above 100 pounds for gloves and sword-knots. . . ." My Lord drives by, and the Mercer makes his low bow to his Honour. "Ah, Jack," says he, "there's my velvet hammer-cloths: would I had let my wife have made cushions of them. . . ."[9]

The man who could throw off dialogue of this penetrating kind in 1706 was ready in one important respect for the writing of fiction. More recently he had come even nearer to fiction in the prose dialogues

---

[7] G. A. Aitken, "Defoe's Birth and Marriage," *Athenaeum,* II (1890), 257.

[8] On 1 Nov. 1718 *Read's Journal* contained a sneering reference to "the little art he is truly master of, of forging a story, and imposing it on the world for truth."

[9] *Review,* III, 31.

of *The Family Instructor,* in which for the purposes of moral instruction he had created a number of characters and set them talking to and at each other.

Yet it would be wrong to suggest that *Robinson Crusoe* was not a very real innovation for Defoe. Not the least astonishing thing about it is the way in which he does something that one might have thought almost impossible for him—loses his own robust personality in one of his own invention. True, there is something of Defoe, an indissoluble element, remaining in Moll Flanders and Roxana, Colonel Jack and Captain Singleton, Robinson Crusoe and the Cavalier; but though all those characters speak in a voice that has some resemblance to Daniel Defoe's, they are not just so many projections of his own personality. They are authentic individuals, with something of the strong smell of Defoe still clinging to them.

Even here, however, there was a precedent for what he was now doing. One of the most persistent pleasures in Defoe's life was make-believe, or, more particularly, the impersonation of some other character. Whether he and his two sisters played at this sort of thing when they were children—"You be the Queen, and I'll be Sir Walter Raleigh"—one need not inquire; but his love of playing parts had appeared long before he ever thought of turning to fiction. In 1698 he had effectively impersonated a humble citizen in *The Poor Man's Plea,* and in 1702 he had reproduced with devastating success in his *Shortest Way* the voice of a high-flying divine. One is reminded of the small boy walking with exaggerated steps and gestures close behind some unsuspecting adult. Later, Defoe had enjoyed playing the part of a Quaker in various pamphlets, and among his other achievements of this kind he had successfully forged the memoirs of M. Mesnager. From that point to the identification of himself with a shipwrecked sailor or a reformed thief no great step was necessary. . . .

It is here, indeed, that his claims to being an artist, so grudgingly admitted by some of his biographers, become most apparent. He took a quite un-puritanical delight in experience for its own sake. He enjoyed the mere variety of human life, the bustle of active people, the shopkeeper scratching his head with his pen, the fine lady cheapening a piece of silk, the beggar limping by on his crutches, the stir and commotion of market-day in a small town, the forest of shipping on the river at Gravesend. For all his Puritanism—and even when he is writing in his most practical and improving manner—those things keep breaking in. There is a striking example as early as the *Essay upon Projects.*[10] Defoe is condemning the practice of swearing, only

[10] I take this example from Dr. R. G. Stamm (*Philological Quarterly,* July 1936, p. 236) who uses it to make this point.

too common among the polite gentlemen of the day. The point is perfectly clear; every one knows what he means by swearing. But Defoe cannot resist one little illustration. He imagines two gentlemen greeting one another:

> "Jack, God damn me, Jack, how do'st do, thou little dear son of a whore? How hast thou done this long time, by God?" and then they kiss; and the other, as lewd as himself, goes on: "Dear Tom, I am glad to see thee, with all my heart; let me die. Come, let us go take a bottle; we must not part so; prithee let's go and be drunk, by God."

Here, in fact, is a bit of real life, a brief transcript from the actual: it gets into the *Essay upon Projects,* not because Defoe the Puritan thinks it ought to be there, but because it has occurred to the mind of Defoe the artist, and he cannot persuade himself to leave it out.

Symbolic Elements in *Robinson Crusoe*

by *Edwin B. Benjamin*

Although Defoe claimed in the *Serious Reflections* that *Robinson Crusoe* was in part an allegory of his own life,[1] attempts to connect details in the book with specific experiences in the life of Defoe have not been found convincing.[2] Complicated as the connection is between Defoe's life and his works, I believe that the claim may yet be found valid if we look at the book as a symbolic account of a spiritual experience rather than a kind of cipher of its author's life.[3] It is quite possible that the symbolism is by no means a part of Defoe's intention; as his imagination warmed to its task, the story began to take on its symbolic overtones, and his later comment is merely an attempt to defend himself against the charges of trying to pass off fiction as fact.

Allegory seems to have been always congenial to the Puritan mind as a legitimate province in which the imagination might exercise it-

Edwin B. Benjamin, "*Symbolic Elements in* Robinson Crusoe," Philological Quarterly, *XXX* (*October 1951*), *206–11. Reprinted by permission of The University of Iowa.*

[1] Daniel Defoe, *Serious Reflections . . . of Robinson Crusoe,* in G. A. Aitken ed. *Romances and Narratives of Daniel Defoe* (London: J. M. Dent and Co., 1895), III, x–xi.

[2] Most of the discussion of this point has revolved around the question of whether or not events in *Robinson Crusoe* refer to specific events in the life of Defoe. William Lee [*Daniel Defoe* (London: John Camden Hotten, 1869) I, 299] and Thomas Wright [*The Life of Daniel Defoe* (London: C. J. Farncombe and Sons Ltd., 1931), pp. 244–47] accept Defoe's word generally; Mr. G. Parker ["The Allegory of *Robinson Crusoe*," *History*, X (1925), 11–25] works out the allegory in a more detailed fashion. Among those who deny that the novel is allegorical—though most agree with Saintsbury that such a theory "cannot be absolutely pooh-poohed"—are William Minto [*Daniel Defoe* (New York: Harper and Brothers, 1879), p. 146], G. A. Aitken (*op. cit.,* I, lv–lvii), Paul Geissler [*Defoes Theorie über Robinson Crusoe* (Halle: 1896), pp. 10–13], James Moffatt ["The Religion of *Robinson Crusoe*," *Contemporary Review*, CXV (1919), 665], and Arthur Wellesley Secord [*Studies in the Narrative Method of Defoe* (University of Illinois: 1924), p. 22].

[3] This is generally the position of M. Paul Dottin, who calls Defoe a Bunyan "en costume laïque" [*Daniel Defoe et Ses Romans* (Paris: Les Presses Universitaires de France, 1924), p. 327]. My analysis, however, attempts to go farther than that of M. Dottin in exploring less conscious levels of meaning.

self;[4] and although at times in the eighteenth century it came to be
looked down upon as a rather crude vehicle of literary expression, it
continued longer as a vital tradition in the dissenting milieu in which
Defoe's mind was molded than in more advanced intellectual and
literary circles. Defoe can hardly have been unaffected by the forces that
shaped Bunyan and that accounted for the continued popularity of his
allegories. It is perhaps surprising that in view of his background we
do not find more evidences of allegory in the work of Defoe.

Robinson Crusoe is far more than the account of a practical man's
adjustment to life on a deserted island. Side by side with Crusoe's
physical conquest of nature is his struggle to conquer himself and to
find God. It is really a conversion story, like that of Augustine or
Baxter, with the classic symptoms of supernatural guidance (in this
case in a dream), penitential tears, and Biblical text. Despite repeated
signs and warnings, Crusoe only gradually awakens to the necessity for
salvation; and it is not until in his illness he stumbles to the tobacco
box and comes upon the Bible that he crosses the hump. The final stage
is his realization that his deliverance from the island is unimportant
in comparison with his deliverance from sin through the mercy of God.

> Now I began to construe the words mentioned above, *Call on me, and
> I will deliver you,* in a different sense from what I had ever done
> before; for then I had no notion of any thing being call'd deliverance,
> but my being deliver'd from the captivity I was in; . . . but now I
> learn'd to take it in another sense. Now I look'd back upon my past
> life with such horrour, and my sins appear'd so dreadful, that my soul
> sought nothing of God but deliverance from the load of guilt that
> bore down all my comfort: as for my solitary life, it was nothing; I
> did not so much pray to be deliver'd from it, or think of it; it was all of
> no consideration in comparison to this.[5]

From this point on, his mind is essentially at peace, and the remainder
of his autobiography is in the nature of an account of the due rewards
and powers of the man who has been saved.

Although Defoe's Christianity is at times fairly materialistic,[6] especially in comparison with that of Augustine, Bunyan or Baxter, the
account of Crusoe's conversion has a peculiar force and intensity to it

[4] Yvor Winters, for instance, [*Maule's Curse* (Norfolk, Connecticut: New Direc-
tions, 1938), pp. 4–11] discusses this point at some length.

[5] Daniel Defoe, *Robinson Crusoe* (London: J. M. Dent and Sons, 1945), p. 72.

[6] Critics vary as to whether the Christianity in *Robinson Crusoe* is organic or
merely a conventional sugar-coating for a pious public. Although I am inclined to
agree with Moffatt (article cited) that it is the former, able presentations of the
opposite point of view can be found in Hans W. Hausermann's "Life and Thought
in *Robinson Crusoe*" [*RES*, XI (1935), 299–312, 439–56] and Rudolf G. Stamm's
"Daniel Defoe: an Artist in the Puritan Tradition" [*PQ*, XV (1936), 225–45].

that tempts one into believing it of some greater than ordinary personal significance to Defoe. It is indicative, I think, that as soon as Crusoe gets back to Europe, he sheds his Christianity like an old cloak and pursues his complacent way with only the most perfunctory expressions of gratitude to his Creator and Preserver (e.g., the scene in the Pyrenees when he is attacked by wolves). But whatever the personal associations of the story to Defoe, at least a part of the effectiveness of the novel is due to the way in which the parallel struggles set off and suggest one another. Some of the details of Crusoe's struggle with nature seem to symbolize his spiritual quest, though perhaps not intentionally on the part of Defoe. One notices that many of these are among the most emphatic and memorable incidents of the novel.

The main outline of Crusoe's story lends itself readily to allegorization. Given the notion of life as a voyage, which is at least as old as patristic commentaries on the *Aeneid,* both storm and desert island, punishment and proving ground, are logical corollaries. Contemporary use of some of these ideas can be found, for instance, in Matthew Green's witty and urbane *The Spleen.*

> Thus, thus I steer my bark, and sail
> On even keel with gentle gale;
> At helm I make my reason sit,
> My crew of passions all submit.
> If dark and blustering prove some nights,
> Philosophy puts forth her lights;
> Experience holds the cautious glass,
> To shun the breakers, as I pass, . . .
> And once in seven years I'm seen
> At Bath or Tunbridge to careen.
> Though pleased to see the dolphins play,
> I mind my compass and my way. . . .
> I make (may heaven propitious send
> Such wind and weather to the end)
> Neither becalmed nor over-blown,
> Life's voyage to the world unknown.[7]

However, it should be emphasized that the distinctive feature of *Crusoe* is that which is apparently original with Defoe, the detailed account of Crusoe's adjustment to the island.

By no means all the details of the novel are allegorical. Some of these I have chosen may be found unconvincing, the well-disposed reader may wish to add others; but at least this will be a start toward

[7] Matthew Green, *The Spleen,* ll. 814–19, 824–27, 832–35. *The Spleen* appeared posthumously in 1737.

isolating one of the elements that make the book such an appealing one.

The geography of the island is conceived in moral terms. The side of the island on which Crusoe lands and where he establishes his "home," as he calls it, although it affords a better prospect of the ocean, is less favored naturally than the other side that he explores later and where he builds his "bower." The latter yields not only a greater variety of fruits—aloes, limes, wild sugar cane, grapes—but a more numerous fauna. Goats abound in the rich meadows, also hares and fox-like creatures, and on the shore a great profusion of turtles, which are something of a rarity on the other side of the island. Crusoe is tempted to move, but decides against it—wisely, as it turns out; for the shore where the turtles can be found is the one where the cannibals are accustomed to land for their inhuman feasts. Also, the richness proves to be largely illusory. Crusoe doesn't dare eat the grapes until dried, for fear of flux; a batch he gathers and leaves overnight are "trod to pieces" and spread about by some "wild creatures"; the goats, though more numerous, are harder to catch because of lack of cover. In a curious passage in his second trip he describes descending into a large wooded valley where he becomes lost for several days in the forests and in a haze that springs up.

It is difficult not to sense allegory at work behind all this. Turtle, as in Pope and Fielding, is a symbol of luxurious living; the grapes are harder to fix, though there may be Biblical overtones here; and the hot misty forest has suggestions of sloth and lassitude: ". . . and then by easy journies I turn'd homeward, the weather being exceeding hot, and my gun, ammunition, hatchet, and other things very heavy." [8] Since these experiences happen to Crusoe on his two exploratory trips shortly after his conversion, the thither side of the island becomes to him, like Egypt to the Israelites on the march to Canaan, a temptation to be resisted.

Fundamentally, the temptation to move is an appeal to a species of pride, not to remain where he had been cast up by divine Providence,[9] but to go whoring after false gods. When it comes to attempting to escape from the island entirely, however, which presumably he must not do until a sign has been given, Crusoe shows that he is not proof against this sin. In his first effort, pride acts to blind his reason; he selects for his *periagua* a cedar so large (there is a significant reference to the temple of Solomon at this point[10]) that when fashioned into a vessel, it cannot be launched by one man. Yet despite this warning he persists,

---

[8] *Robinson Crusoe*, p. 82.

[9] *Ibid.*, p. 80.

[10] *Ibid.*, p. 93.

builds a second boat, and, in maneuvering about the island, is almost swept away by currents to certain death. It is only then that Crusoe realizes where his unwillingness to accept his lot has led him; falling on his knees, he thanks God for his preservation and resolves "to lay aside all thoughts of my deliverance by my boat." [11]

This incident acts as a turning point in Crusoe's career; from here on he makes no major mistakes, though he is capable of certain indiscreet plans in reference to the cannibals in the long course of his preoccupation with them.

Generally, the symbolism is clustered around the conversion. The peculiar effectiveness of the descriptions of the shoots of barley and the making of the earthen pot is probably due to their symbolic value in the religious context. Crusoe sheds tears at the realization that the stalks are "perfect green barley," [12] and for the first time begins to reflect seriously on God's providence. Clearly, they are the seeds of grace stirring in his heart and sending forth their first tender sprouts. Similarly, Crusoe's ultimate success in fashioning an earthen pot after certain false starts is analogous to his ultimate success in attaining a spiritual goal.[13] In a sense Crusoe is the pot himself. Several times he has been brought to the fire, but nothing had come of it. Finally, however, his trials redouble (fresh fuel is brought to the fire), he glows clear red, and emerges a serviceable, if not handsome pipkin of the Lord. The analogy may seem far-fetched at first; but one should remember, in addition to the fact that the very intensity of these descriptions suggest a special meaning for them, that dissenting circles were accustomed to think and to express themselves in terms of "chosen vessels" and seeds of grace or doctrine.

Other incidents may be susceptible of such an interpretation: the goatskin clothes he makes after his old ones wear out may be the new armor of faith,[14] and the elaborate system of defense that Crusoe establishes on the island may suggest the invulnerability of the true believer; but the four examples I have chosen are the most obvious in respect to both their nature and their position in the narrative.

[11] *Ibid.*, p. 104.

[12] *Ibid.*, p. 58.

[13] *Ibid.*, p. 89. Virginia Woolf ["Robinson Crusoe" in *Second Common Reader* (New York: Harcourt, Brace and Company, 1932), pp. 50–58] makes the earthen pot a focal point of her essay. Reprinted pp. 19–24 above.

[14] *Ibid.*, p. 109. The suit of new armor in Governor Bellingham's hall [Nathaniel Hawthorne, *Scarlet Letter* (New York: Rinehart and Company, 1947), p. 99] has a symbolic value of this sort. See the analysis of this passage in Winters (*op. cit.*, pp. 12–3).

Robinson Crusoe, Individualism and the Novel

by Ian Watt

[*1. Robinson Crusoe reduces all human relationships to economic advantage*]

Robinson Crusoe has been very appropriately used by many economic theorists as their illustration of *homo economicus*. Just as "the body politic" was the symbol of the communal way of thought typical of previous societies, so "economic man" symbolised the new outlook of individualism in its economic aspect. Adam Smith has been charged with the invention; actually, the concept is much older, but it is natural that it should have come to the fore as an abstraction expressing the individualism of the economic system as a whole only when the individualism of that system itself had reached an advanced stage of development.

That Robinson Crusoe, like Defoe's other main characters, Moll Flanders, Roxana, Colonel Jacque and Captain Singleton, is an embodiment of economic individualism hardly needs demonstration. All Defoe's heroes pursue money, which he characteristically called "the general denominating article in the world";[1] and they pursue it very methodically according to the profit and loss book-keeping which Max Weber considered to be the distinctive technical feature of modern capitalism.[2] Defoe's heroes, we observe, have no need to learn this technique; whatever the circumstances of their birth and education, they have it in their blood, and keep us more fully informed of their present stocks of money and commodities than any other characters in fiction. Crusoe's book-keeping conscience, indeed, has established an effective priority over his other thoughts and emotions; when his

From Ian Watt, The Rise of the Novel: Studies in Defoe, Richardson and Fielding *(Berkeley and Los Angeles: University of California Press, 1957), pp. 63–74, 85–92. Reprinted by permission of the publisher.*

[1] *Review,* III (1706), No. 3.
[2] *The Theory of Social and Economic Organisation,* trans. Henderson and Parsons (New York, 1947), pp. 186–202.

Lisbon steward offers him 160 moidores to alleviate his momentary difficulties on return, Crusoe relates: "I could hardly refrain from tears while he spoke; in short, I took 100 of the moidores, and called for a pen and ink to give him a receipt for them." [3]

Book-keeping is but one aspect of a central theme in the modern social order. Our civilisation as a whole is based on individual contractual relationships, as opposed to the unwritten, traditional and collective relationships of previous societies; and the idea of contract played an important part in the theoretical development of political individualism. It had featured prominently in the fight against the Stuarts, and it was enshrined in Locke's political system. Locke, indeed, thought that contractual relationships were binding even in the state of nature.[4] . . .

But the primacy of the economic motive, and an innate reverence for book-keeping and the law of contract are by no means the only matters in which Robinson Crusoe is a symbol of the processes associated with the rise of economic individualism. The hypostasis of the economic motive logically entails a devaluation of other modes of thought, feeling and action: the various forms of traditional group relationship, the family, the guild, the village, the sense of nationality —all are weakened, and so, too, are the competing claims of non-economic individual achievement and enjoyment, ranging from spiritual salvation to the pleasures of recreation.[5]

This inclusive reordering of the components of human society tends to occur wherever industrial capitalism becomes the dominant force in the economic structure,[6] and it naturally became evident particularly early in England. By the middle of the eighteenth century, indeed, it had already become something of a commonplace. Goldsmith, for instance, thus described the concomitants of England's vaunted freedom in *The Traveller* (1764):

> That independence Britons prize too high,
> Keeps man from man, and breaks the social tie;
> The self-dependent lordlings stand alone,
> All claims that bind and sweeten life unknown;
> Here by the bonds of nature feebly held,
> Minds combat minds, repelling and repell'd . . .

[3] *The Life and Strange Surprizing Adventures of Robinson Crusoe,* ed. Aitken (London, 1902), p. 316.

[4] Second treatise, "Essay concerning . . . Civil Government," sect. 14.

[5] See Max Weber, *The Protestant Ethic and the Spirit of Capitalism,* trans. Parsons (London, 1930), pp. 59–76; *Social and Economic Organisation,* pp. 341–54.

[6] See, for example, Robert Redfield, *Folk Culture of Yucatan* (Chicago, 1941), pp. 338–69.

Nor this the worst. As nature's ties decay,
As duty, love, and honour fail to sway,
Fictitious bonds, the bonds of wealth and law,
Still gather strength, and force unwilling awe.[7]

Unlike Goldsmith, Defoe was not a professed enemy of the new order—quite the reverse; nevertheless there is much in *Robinson Crusoe* that bears out Goldsmith's picture, as can be seen in Defoe's treatment of such group relationships as the family or the nation.

For the most part, Defoe's heroes either have no family, like Moll Flanders, Colonel Jacque and Captain Singleton, or leave it at an early age never to return, like Roxana and Robinson Crusoe. Not too much importance can be attached to this fact, since adventure stories demand the absence of conventional social ties. Still, in *Robinson Crusoe* at least, the hero has a home and family, and leaves them for the classic reason of *homo economicus*—that it is necessary to better his economic condition. "Something fatal in that propension of nature" calls him to the sea and adventure, and against "settling to business" in the station to which he is born—"the upper station of low life"; and this despite the panegyric which his father makes of that condition. Later he sees this lack of "confined desires," this dissatisfaction with "the state wherein God and Nature has placed" him, as his "original sin." [8] At the time, however, the argument between his parents and himself is a debate, not about filial duty or religion, but about whether going or staying is likely to be the most advantageous course materially: both sides accept the economic argument as primary. And, of course, Crusoe actually gains by his "original sin," and becomes richer than his father was.

Crusoe's "original sin" is really the dynamic tendency of capitalism itself, whose aim is never merely to maintain the *status quo,* but to transform it incessantly. Leaving home, improving on the lot one was born to, is a vital feature of the individualist pattern of life. It may be regarded as the economic and social embodiment of the "uneasiness" which Locke had made the centre of his system of motivation,[9] an uneasiness whose existence was, in the very opposite outlook of Pascal, the index of the enduring misery of mortal man. "All the unhappiness of men arises from one single fact, that they cannot stay quietly in their own room" Pascal had written.[10] Defoe's hero is far from agreeing. Even when he is old, Crusoe tells us how ". . . nothing

[7] Ll. 339–52.
[8] *Life,* pp. 2–6, 216.
[9] *Human Understanding,* Bk. II, ch. 21, sects. xxxi–lx.
[10] *Pensées,* No. 139.

else offering, and finding that really stirring about and trading, the profit being so great, and, as I may say, certain, had more pleasure in it, and more satisfaction to the mind, than sitting still, which, to me especially, was the unhappiest part of life." [11] So, in the *Farther Adventures,* Crusoe sets out on yet another lucrative Odyssey.

The fundamental tendency of economic individualism, then, prevents Crusoe from paying much heed to the ties of family, whether as a son or a husband. This is in direct contradiction to the great stress which Defoe lays on the social and religious importance of the family in his didactic works such as the *Family Instructor;* but his novels reflect not theory but practice, and they accord these ties a very minor, and on the whole obstructive, role.

Rational scrutiny of one's own economic interest may lead one to be as little bound by national as by family ties. Defoe certainly valued individuals and countries alike primarily on their economic merits. Thus one of his most patriotic utterances takes the characteristic form of claiming that his compatriots have a greater productive output per hour than the workmen of any other country.[12] Crusoe, we notice, whom Walter de la Mare has justly called Defoe's Elective Affinity, [13] shows xenophobia mainly where the economic virtues are absent. When they are present—as in the Spanish Governor, a French papist priest, a faithful Portuguese factor—his praise is unstinted. On the other hand, he condemns many Englishmen, such as his English settlers on the island, for their lack of industry. Crusoe, one feels, is not bound to his country by sentimental ties, any more than to his family; he is satisfied by people, whatever their nationality, who are good to do business with; and he feels, like Moll Flanders, that "with money in the pocket one is at home anywhere." [14]

What might at first appear to place *Robinson Crusoe* in the somewhat special category of "Travel and Adventure" does not, then, altogether do so. The plot's reliance on travel does tend to allot *Robinson Crusoe* a somewhat peripheral position in the novel's line of development, since it removes the hero from his usual setting in a stable and cohesive pattern of social relations. But Crusoe is not a mere footloose adventurer, and his travels, like his freedom from social ties, are merely somewhat extreme cases of tendencies that are normal in modern society as a whole, since, by making the pursuit of gain a primary motive, economic individualism has much increased the mobility of the individual. More specifically, Robinson Crusoe's career

[11] *Farther Adventures of Robinson Crusoe,* ed. Aitken (London, 1902), p. 214.

[12] *A Plan of the English Commerce* (Oxford, 1928), pp. 28, 31–32.

[13] *Desert Islands and Robinson Crusoe* (London, 1930), p. 7.

[14] *Moll Flanders,* ed. Aitken (London, 1902), I, 186.

is based, as modern scholarship has shown,[15] on some of the innumerable volumes which recounted the exploits of those voyagers who had done so much in the sixteenth century to assist the development of capitalism by providing the gold, slaves and tropical products on which trade expansion depended; and who had continued the process in the seventeenth century by developing the colonies and world markets on which the future progress of capitalism depended.

Defoe's plot, then, expresses some of the most important tendencies of the life of his time, and it is this which sets his hero apart from most of the travellers in literature. Robinson Crusoe is not, like Autolycus, a commercial traveller rooted in an extended but still familiar locality; nor is he, like Ulysses, an unwilling voyager trying to get back to his family and his native land: profit is Crusoe's only vocation, and the whole world is his territory.

The primacy of individual economic advantage has tended to diminish the importance of personal as well as group relationships, and especially of those based on sex; for sex, as Weber pointed out,[16] being one of the strongest non-rational factors in human life, is one of the strongest potential menaces to the individual's rational pursuit of economic ends, and it has therefore, as we shall see, been placed under particularly strong controls in the ideology of industrial capitalism.

Romantic love has certainly had no greater antagonist among the novelists than Defoe. Even sexual satisfaction—where he speaks of it —tends to be minimised; he protested in *The Review,* for example, that "the Trifle called Pleasure in it" was "not worth the Repentance." [17] As to marriage, his attitude is complicated by the fact that economic and moral virtue in the male is no guarantee of a profitable matrimonial investment: on his colony "as it often happens in the world (what the wise ends of God's Providence are in such a disposition of things I cannot say), the two honest fellows had the two worst wives, and the three reprobates, that were scarce worth hanging . . . had three clever, diligent, careful and ingenious wives." [18] His puzzled parenthesis bears eloquent testimony to the seriousness with which he views this flaw in the rationality of Province.

It is not surprising, therefore, that love plays little part in Crusoe's own life, and that even the temptations of sex are excluded from the scene of his greatest triumphs, the island. When Crusoe does notice the lack of "society" there, he prays for the solace of company, but

[15] See especially A. W. Secord, *Studies in the Narrative Method of Defoe* (Urbana, 1924).

[16] Weber, *Essays in Sociology,* trans. Gerth and Mills (New York, 1946), p. 350.

[17] I (1705), No. 92.

[18] *Farther Adventures,* p. 78.

we observe that what he desires is a male slave.[19] Then, with Friday, he enjoys an idyll without benefit of woman—a revolutionary departure from the traditional expectations aroused by desert islands from the *Odyssey* to the *New Yorker*.

When eventually Crusoe returns to civilisation, sex is still strictly subordinated to business. Only when his financial position has been fully secured by a further voyage does he marry; and all he tells us of this supreme human adventure is that it was "not either to my disadvantage or dissatisfaction." This, the birth of three children, and his wife's death, however, comprise only the early part of a sentence, which ends with plans for a further voyage.[20]

Women have only one important role to play, and that is economic. When Crusoe's colonists draw lots for five women, we are gleefully informed that:

> He that drew to choose first . . . took her that was reckoned the homeliest and eldest of the five, which made mirth enough among the rest . . . but the fellow considered better than any of them, that it was application and business that they were to expect assistance in as much as anything else; and she proved the best wife of all the parcel.[21]

"The best wife of all the parcel." The language of commerce here reminds us that Dickens once decided on the basis of Defoe's treatment of women that he must have been "a precious dry and disagreeable article himself." [22]

The same devaluation of non-economic factors can be seen in Crusoe's other personal relationships. He treats them all in terms of their commodity value. The clearest case is that of Xury, the Moorish boy who helped him to escape from slavery and on another occasion offered to prove his devotion by sacrificing his own life. Crusoe very properly resolves "to love him ever after" and promises "to make him a great man." But when chance leads them to the Portuguese Captain, who offers Crusoe sixty pieces of eight—twice Judas's figure—he cannot resist the bargain, and sells Xury into slavery. He has momentary scruples, it is true, but they are cheaply satisfied by securing a promise from the new owner to "set him free in ten years if he turn Christian." Remorse later supervenes, but only when the tasks of his island life make manpower more valuable to him than money.[23]

Crusoe's relations with Man Friday are similarly egocentric. He does

[19] *Life*, pp. 208–10, 225.
[20] *Life*, p. 341.
[21] *Farther Adventures*, p. 77.
[22] John Forster, *Life of Charles Dickens*, revised Ley (London, 1928), p. 611 n.
[23] *Life*, pp. 27, 34–36, 164.

not ask him his name, but gives him one. Even in language—the medium whereby human beings may achieve something more than animal relationships with each other, as Crusoe himself wrote in his *Serious Reflections*[24]—Crusoe is a strict utilitarian. "I likewise taught him to say Yes and No," [25] he tells us; but Friday still speaks pidgin English at the end of their long association, as Defoe's contemporary critic Charles Gildon pointed out.[26]

Yet Crusoe regards the relationship as ideal. He is "as perfectly and completely happy if any such thing as complete happiness can be found in a sublunary state." [27] A functional silence, broken only by an occasional "No, Friday," or an abject "Yes, Master," is the golden music of Crusoe's *île joyeuse*. It seems that man's social nature, his need for friendship and understanding, is wholly satisfied by the righteous bestowal or grateful receipt, of benevolent but not undemanding patronage. It is true that later, as with Xury, Crusoe promises himself "to do something considerable" for his servant, "if he outlive me." Fortunately, no such sacrifice is called for, as Friday dies at sea, to be rewarded only by a brief word of obituary compassion.[28]

[*2. Robinson Crusoe recreates a primitive crafts economy*]

If Robinson Crusoe's character depends very largely on the psychological and social orientations of economic individualism, the appeal of his adventures to the reader seems mainly to derive from the effects of another important concomitant of modern capitalism, economic specialisation.

The division of labour has done much to make the novel possible: partly because the more specialised the social and economic structure, the greater the number of significant differences of character, attitude and experience in contemporary life which the novelist can portray, and which are of interest to his readers; partly because, by increasing the amount of leisure, economic specialisation provides the kind of mass audience with which the novel is associated; and partly because this specialisation creates particular needs in that audience which the novel satisfies. Such, at least, was the general view of T. H. Green:

[24] *Serious Reflections during the Life and Surprising Adventures of Robinson Crusoe*, ed. Aitken (London, 1902), p. 66.
[25] *Life*, p. 229.
[26] *Robinson Crusoe Examin'd and Criticis'd*, ed. Dottin (London and Paris, 1923), pp. 70, 78, 118.
[27] *Life*, pp. 245–46.
[28] *Farther Adventures*, pp. 133, 177–80.

"In the progressive division of labour, while we become more useful as citizens, we seem to lose our completeness as men . . . the perfect organisation of modern society removes the excitement of adventure and the occasion for independent effort. There is less of human interest to touch us within our calling. . . ." "The alleviation" of this situation, Green concluded, "is to be found in the newspaper and the novel." [29]

It is very likely that the lack of variety and stimulation in the daily task as a result of economic specialisation is largely responsible for the unique dependence of the individual in our culture upon the substitute experiences provided by the printing press, particularly in the forms of journalism and the novel. *Robinson Crusoe,* however, is a much more direct illustration of Green's thesis, since much of its appeal obviously depends on the quality of the "occasions for independent effort" in the economic realm which it offers Defoe's hero, efforts which the reader can share vicariously. The appeal of these efforts is surely a measure of the depth of the deprivations involved by economic specialisation, deprivations whose far-reaching nature is suggested by the way our civilisation has reintroduced some of the basic economic processes as therapeutic recreations: in gardening, home-weaving, pottery, camping, woodwork and keeping pets, we can all participate in the character-forming satisfactions which circumstances force on Defoe's hero; and like him, demonstrate what we would not otherwise know, that "by making the most rational judgement of things, every man may be in time master of every mechanic art." [30]

Defoe was certainly aware of how the increasing economic specialisation which was a feature of the life of his time had made most of the "mechanic arts" alien to the experience of his readers. When Crusoe makes bread, for instance, he reflects that " 'Tis a little wonderful and what I believe few people have thought much upon, viz., the strange multitude of little things necessary in the providing, procuring, curing, dressing, making and finishing this one article of bread." [31] Defoe's description goes on for seven pages, pages that would have been of little interest to people in mediaeval or Tudor society, who saw this and other basic economic processes going on daily in their own households. But by the early eighteenth century, as Kalm reported, most women did not "bake, because there is a baker in every parish or village," [32] and Defoe could therefore expect his readers to be interested in the

[29] "Estimate of the Value and Influence of Works of Fiction in Modern Times," *Works,* ed. Nettleship, III, 40.

[30] *Life,* p. 74.

[31] *Life,* p. 130.

[32] *Account of His Visit to England,* p. 326.

very detailed descriptions of the economic life which comprise such an important and memorable part of his narrative.

Robinson Crusoe, of course, does not deal with the actual economic life of Defoe's own time and place. It would be somewhat contrary to the facts of economic life under the division of labour to show the average individual's manual labour as interesting or inspiring; to take Adam Smith's famous example of the division of labour in *The Wealth of Nations,*[33] the man who performs one of the many separate operations in the manufacture of a pin is unlikely to find his task as absorbing and interesting as Crusoe does. So Defoe sets back the economic clock, and takes his hero to a primitive environment, where labour can be presented as varied and inspiring, and where it has the further significant difference from the pin-maker's at home that there is an absolute equivalence between individual effort and individual reward. This was the final change from contemporary economic conditions which was necessary to enable Defoe to give narrative expression to the ideological counterpart of the Division of Labour, the Dignity of Labour.

The creed of the dignity of labour is not wholly modern: in classical times the Cynics and Stoics had opposed the denigration of manual labour which is a necessary part of a slaveowning society's scale of values; and later, Christianity, originally associated mainly with slaves and the poor, had done much to remove the odium on manual labour. The idea, however, was only fully developed in the modern period, presumably because its compensatory affirmation became the more necessary as the development of economic specialisation made manual labour more stultifying; and the creed itself is closely associated with the advent of Protestantism. Calvinism in particular tended to make its adherents forget the idea that labour was God's punishment for Adam's disobedience, by emphasising the very different idea that untiring stewardship of the material gifts of God was a paramount religious and ethical obligation.[34]

The quality of Crusoe's stewardship cannot be doubted; he allows himself little time for rest, and even the advent of new manpower—Friday's—is a signal, not for relaxation, but for expanded production. Defoe clearly belongs to the tradition of Ascetic Protestantism. He had written much that sounds like the formulations of Weber, Troeltsch and Tawney; in Dickory Cronke's aphorism, for example: "When you find yourself sleepy in a morning, rouse yourself, and consider that you

[33] Bk. I, ch. 1.
[34] See Ernst Troeltsch, *Social Teaching of the Christian Churches,* trans. Wyon (London, 1931), I, 119; II, 589; Tawney, *Religion and the Rise of Capitalism* (London, 1948), pp. 197–270.

are born to business, and that in doing good in your generation, you answer your character and act like a man." [35] He had even—with a certain sophistic obtuseness—propounded the view that the pursuit of economic utility was quite literally an imitation of Christ: "Usefulness being the great pleasure, and justly deem'd by all good men the truest and noblest end of life, in which men come nearest to the character of our B. Saviour, who went about doing good." [36]

Defoe's attitude here exhibits a confusion of religious and material values to which the Puritan gospel of the dignity of labour was peculiarly liable: once the highest spiritual values had been attached to the performance of the daily task, the next step was for the autonomous individual to regard his achievements as a quasi-divine mastering of the environment. It is likely that this secularisation of the Calvinist conception of stewardship was of considerable importance for the rise of the novel. *Robinson Crusoe* is certainly the first novel in the sense that it is the first fictional narrative in which an ordinary person's daily activities are the centre of continuous literary attention. These activities, it is true, are not seen in a wholly secular light; but later novelists could continue Defoe's serious concern with man's worldly doings without placing them in a religious framework. It is therefore likely that the Puritan conception of the dignity of labour helped to bring into being the novel's general premise that the individual's daily life is of sufficient importance and interest to be the proper subject of literature.

[3. Robinson Crusoe *as myth*]

Robinson Crusoe falls most naturally into place, not with other novels, but with the great myths of Western civilisation, with *Faust, Don Juan* and *Don Quixote*. All these have as their basic plots, their enduring images, a single-minded pursuit by the protagonist of one of the characteristic desires of Western man. Each of their heroes embodies an *arete* and a *hubris,* an exceptional prowess and a vitiating excess, in spheres of action that are particularly important in our culture. Don Quixote, the impetuous generosity and the limiting blindness of chivalric idealism; Don Juan, pursuing and at the same time tormented by the idea of boundless experience of women; Faustus, the great knower, his curiosity always unsatisfied, and therefore damned. Crusoe, of course, seems to insist that he is not of their company; *they* are very exceptional people, whereas anyone would do what *he*

---

[35] *The Dumb Philosopher* (1719), ed. Scott (London, 1841), p. 21.
[36] *The Case of Protestant Dissenters in Carolina,* 1706, p. 5.

did, in the circumstances. Yet he too has an exceptional prowess; he can manage quite on his own. And he has an excess: his inordinate egocentricity condemns him to isolation wherever he is.

The egocentricity, one might say, is forced on him, because he is cast away on an island. But it is also true that his character is throughout courting its fate and it merely happens that the island offers the fullest opportunity for him to realise three associated tendencies of modern civilisation—absolute economic, social and intellectual freedom for the individual.

It was Crusoe's realisation of intellectual freedom which made Rousseau propose the book as "the one book that teaches all that books can teach" for the education of Émile; he argued that "the surest way to raise oneself above prejudices, and order one's judgement on the real relationship between things, is to put oneself in the place of an isolated man, and to judge of everything as that man would judge of them according to their actual usefulness." [37]

On his island Crusoe also enjoys the absolute freedom from social restrictions for which Rousseau yearned—there are no family ties or civil authorities to interfere with his individual autonomy. Even when he is no longer alone his personal autarchy remains—indeed it is increased: the parrot cries out his master's name; unprompted Friday swears to be his slave for ever; Crusoe toys with the fancy that he is an absolute monarch; and one of his visitors even wonders if he is a god.[38]

Lastly, Crusoe's island gives him the complete *laissez-faire* which economic man needs to realise his aims. At home, market conditions, taxation and problems of the labour supply make it impossible for the individual to control every aspect of production, distribution and exchange. The conclusion is obvious. Follow the call of the wide open places, discover an island that is desert only because it is barren of owners or competitors, and there build your personal Empire with the help of a Man Friday who needs no wages and makes it much easier to support the white man's burden.

Such is the positive and prophetic side of Defoe's story, the side which makes Crusoe an inspiration to economists and educators, and a symbol both for the displaced persons of urban capitalism, such as Rousseau, and for its more practical heroes, the empire builders. Crusoe realises all these ideal freedoms, and in doing so he is undoubtedly a distinctively modern culture-hero. Aristotle, for example, who thought that the man "who is unable to live in society, or who has no need because he is sufficient for himself, must be either a beast or a god," [39]

[37] *Émile, ou De l'éducation* (Paris, 1939), pp. 210, 214.
[38] *Life*, pp. 226, 164, 300, 284.
[39] *Politics*, Bk. I, ch. 2.

would surely have found Crusoe a very strange hero. Perhaps with reason; for it is surely true that the ideal freedoms he achieves are both quite impracticable in the real world and in so far as they can be applied, disastrous for human happiness.

It may be objected that Robinson Crusoe's achievements are credible and wholly convincing. This is so, but only because in his narrative— perhaps as an unconscious victim of what Karl Mannheim has called the "Utopian mentality" which is dominated by its will to action and consequently "turns its back on everything which would shake its belief" [40]—Defoe disregarded two important facts: the social nature of all human economies, and the actual psychological effects of solitude.

The basis for Robinson Crusoe's prosperity, of course, is the original stock of tools which he loots from the shipwreck; they comprise, we are told, "the biggest magazine of all kinds . . . that was ever laid up for one man." [41] So Defoe's hero is not really a primitive nor a proletarian but a capitalist. In the island he owns the freehold of a rich though unimproved estate. Its possession, combined with the stock from the ship, are the miracles which fortify the faith of the supporters of the new economic creed. But only that of the true believers: to the sceptic the classic idyll of free enterprise does not in fact sustain the view that anyone has ever attained comfort and security only by his own efforts. Crusoe is in fact the lucky heir to the labours of countless other individuals; his solitude is the measure, and the price of his luck, since it involves the fortunate decease of all the other potential stockholders; and the shipwreck, far from being a tragic peripety, is the *deus ex machina* which makes it possible for Defoe to present solitary labour, not as an alternative to a death sentence, but as a solution to the perplexities of economic and social reality.

The psychological objection to *Robinson Crusoe* as a pattern of action is also obvious. Just as society has made every individual what he is, so the prolonged lack of society actually tends to make the individual relapse into a straitened primitivism of thought and feeling. In Defoe's sources for *Robinson Crusoe* what actually happened to the castaways was at best uninspiring. At worst, harassed by fear and dogged by ecological degradation, they sank more and more to the level of animals, lost the use of speech, went mad, or died of inanition. One book which Defoe had almost certainly read, *The Voyages and Travels of J. Albert de Mandelslo,* tells of two such cases; of a Frenchman who, after only two years of solitude on Mauritius, tore his clothing to pieces in a fit of madness brought on by a diet of raw tortoise;

[40] *Ideology and Utopia* (London, 1936), p. 36.
[41] *Life,* p. 60.

and of a Dutch seaman on St. Helena who disinterred the body of a buried comrade and set out to sea in the coffin.[42]

These realities of absolute solitude were in keeping with the traditional view of its effects, as expressed by Dr. Johnson: the "solitary mortal," he averred, was "certainly luxurious, probably superstitious, and possibly mad: the mind stagnates for want of employment; grows morbid, and is extinguished like a candle in foul air." [43]

In the story just the opposite happens: Crusoe turns his forsaken estate into a triumph. Defoe departs from psychological probability in order to redeem his picture of man's inexorable solitariness, and it is for this reason that he appeals very strongly to all who feel isolated —and who at times does not? An inner voice continually suggests to us that the human isolation which individualism has fostered is painful and tends ultimately to a life of apathetic animality and mental derangement; Defoe answers confidently that it can be made the arduous prelude to the fuller realisation of every individual's potentialities; and the solitary readers of two centuries of individualism cannot but applaud so convincing an example of making a virtue out of a necessity, so cheering a colouring to that universal image of individualist experience, solitude.

That it is universal—the word that is always to be found inscribed on the other side of the coin of individualism—can hardly be doubted. We have already seen how, although Defoe himself was an optimistic spokesman of the new economic and social order, the unreflecting veracity of his vision as a novelist led him to report many of the less inspiring phenomena associated with economic individualism which tended to isolate man from his family and his country. Modern sociologists have attributed very similar consequences to the other two major trends which are reflected in *Robinson Crusoe*. Max Weber, for example, has shown how the religious individualism of Calvin created among its adherents a historically unprecedented "inner isolation";[44] while Émile Durkheim derived from the division of labour and its associated changes many of the endless conflicts and complexities of the norms of modern society, the *anomie*[45] which sets the individual on his own and, incidentally, provides the novelists with a rich mine of individual and social problems when he portrays the life of his time.

Defoe himself seems to have been much more aware of the larger representativeness of his epic of solitude than is commonly assumed.

[42] See Secord, *Narrative Method of Defoe*, pp. 28–29.
[43] *Thraliana*, ed. Balderston (Oxford, 1951), I, 180.
[44] *Protestant Ethic*, p. 108.
[45] *De la division du travail social*, Bk. II, chs. 1 and 3.

Not wholly aware, since, as we have seen, he departed from its actual economic and psychological effects to make his hero's struggles more cheering than they might otherwise have been; nevertheless Crusoe's most eloquent utterances are concerned with solitude as the universal state of man.

The *Serious Reflections of Robinson Crusoe* (1720) are actually a miscellaneous compilation of religious, moral and thaumaturgic material, and cannot, as a whole, be taken seriously as a part of the story: the volume was primarily put together to cash in on the great success of the first part of the trilogy, *The Life and Strange Surprising Adventures,* and the smaller one of the *Farther Adventures.* There are, however, in the prefaces, and the first essay, "On Solitude," a number of valuable clues as to what, on second thoughts at least, Defoe saw as the meaning of his hero's experiences. . . .

Defoe was himself an isolated and solitary figure in his time; witness the summary of his own life which he wrote in the preface to a 1706 pamphlet, *A Reply to a Pamphlet, Entitled "The Lord Haversham's Vindication of His Speech . . . ,"* where he complains

> how I stand alone in the world, abandoned by those very people that own I have done them service; . . . how, with . . . no helps but my own industry, I have forced misfortune, and reduced them, exclusive of composition, from seventeen to less than five thousand pounds; how, in gaols, in retreats, in all manner of extremities, I have supported myself without the assistance of friends or relations.

"Forcing his way with undiscouraged diligence" is surely the heroism which Crusoe shares with his creator: and in "Robinson Crusoe's Preface" it is this quality which he mentions as the inspiring theme of his book: "Here is invincible patience recommended under the worst of misery, indefatigable application and undaunted resolution under the greatest and most discouraging circumstances."

Having asserted an autobiographical meaning for his story, Defoe goes on to consider the problem of solitude. His discussion is an interesting illustration of Weber's view of the effects of Calvinism. Most of the argument is concerned with the Puritan insistence on the need for the individual to overcome the world in his own soul, to achieve a spiritual solitude without recourse to monasticism. "The business is to get a retired soul," he says, and goes on: "All the parts of a complete solitude are to be as effectually enjoyed, if we please, and sufficient grace assisting, even in the most populous cities, among the hurries of conversation and gallantry of a court, or the noise and business of a camp, as in the deserts of Arabia and Lybia, or in the desolate life of an uninhabited island."

This note, however, occasionally relapses into a more general statement of solitude as an enduring psychological fact: "All reflection is
carried home, and our dear self is, in one respect, the end of living.
Hence man may be properly said to be alone in the midst of crowds and
the hurry of men and business. All the reflections which he makes are
to himself; all that is pleasant he embraces for himself; all that is irk-
some and grievous is tasted but by his own palate." [46] Here the Puritan
insistence on possessing one's soul intact from a sinful world is couched
in terms which suggest a more absolute, secular and personal aliena-
tion from society. Later this echo of the redefined aloneness of Des-
cartes's *solus ipse* modulates into an anguished sense of personal lone-
liness whose overpowering reality moves Defoe to his most urgent and
moving eloquence:

> What are the sorrows of other men to us, and what their joy? Some-
> thing we may be touched indeed with by the power of sympathy, and
> a secret turn of the affections; but all the solid reflection is directed to
> ourselves. Our meditations are all solitude in perfection; our passions
> are all exercised in retirement; we love, we hate, we covet, we enjoy,
> all in privacy and solitude. All that we communicate of those things to
> any other is but for their assistance in the pursuit of our desires; the
> end is at home; the enjoyment, the contemplation, is all solitude and
> retirement; it is for ourselves we enjoy, and for ourselves we suffer.

"We covet, we enjoy, all in privacy and solitude": what really occupies man is something that makes him solitary wherever he is, and
too aware of the interested nature of any relationship with other
human beings to find any consolation there. "All that we communicate
. . . to any other is but for their assistance in the pursuit of our
desires": a rationally conceived self-interest makes a mockery of speech;
and the scene of Crusoe's silent life is not least a Utopia because its
functional silence, broken only by an occasional "Poor Robinson
Crusoe" from the parrot, does not impose upon man's ontological
egocentricity the need to assume a false façade of social intercourse, or
to indulge in the mockery of communication with his fellows.

Robinson Crusoe, then, presents a monitory image of the ultimate
consequences of absolute individualism. But this tendency, like all extreme tendencies, soon provoked a reaction. As soon as man's aloneness
was forced on the attention of mankind, the close and complex nature
of the individual's dependence on society, which had been taken for
granted until it was challenged by individualism, began to receive
much more detailed analysis. Man's essentially social nature, for instance, became one of the main topics of the eighteenth-century

[46] Pp. 7, 15, 2, 2–3.

philosophers; and the greatest of them, David Hume, wrote in the *Treatise of Human Nature* (1739) a passage which might almost have been a refutation of *Robinson Crusoe:*

> We can form no wish which has not a reference to society. . . . Let all the powers and elements of nature conspire to serve and obey one man; let the sun rise and set at his command; the sea and rivers roll as he pleases, and the earth still furnish spontaneously whatever may be useful or agreeable to him; he will still be miserable, till you give him one person at least with whom he may share his happiness, and whose esteem and friendship he may enjoy.[47]

Just as the modern study of society only began once individualism had focussed attention on man's apparent disjunctions from his fellows, so the novel could only begin its study of personal relationships once *Robinson Crusoe* had revealed a solitude that cried aloud for them. Defoe's story is perhaps not a novel in the usual sense since it deals so little with personal relations. But it is appropriate that the tradition of the novel should begin with a work that annihilated the relationships of the traditional social order, and thus drew attention to the opportunity and the need of building up a network of personal relationships on a new and conscious pattern; the terms of the problem of the novel and of modern thought alike were established when the old order of moral and social relationships was shipwrecked, with Robinson Crusoe, by the rising tide of individualism.

[47] Bk. II, pt. 2, sect. v.

Robinson Crusoe

by John Robert Moore

"You are a great traveler, and we honor you as such," said a monk to Mr. Paton during a repast in the refectory; "but the greatest traveler of your country we have heard of was Robinson Crusoe of York, who met with many and strange adventures, but at length, by the blessing of God, returned to his native land."

> "Servia," *Quarterly Review,* CXVII
> (January, 1865), 195, quoting from
> Paton's *Danube and the Adriatic*[1]

The most significant date in Defoe's literary career was April 25, 1719, when the first volume of *Robinson Crusoe* was published. Before that there was no English novel worth the name, and no book (except the Bible) widely accepted among all classes of English and Scottish readers. *The Pilgrim's Progress* had many elements of great fiction; but it was intended as a work of religious instruction, it was meant for humble readers, and for a century it was despised by literary critics. The impact of *Robinson Crusoe* was greater, and in some ways quite different. There were doubts about whether it was a genuine travel book, a fraudulent travel book, or a legitimate work of fiction, so that Defoe resorted to improvisations and equivocations to evade questions about its truth to fact. But the esteem in which it was held in the literary world is shown by the praise it received from Alexander Pope, by its immense influence on *Gulliver's Travels,* and by Dr. Johnson's including it as one of the three books by mere man which anyone would wish longer. Its popularity among the lowest classes of readers was a source of jealousy which sought relief in a pretense of scorn:

From John Robert Moore, Daniel Defoe: Citizen of the Modern World *(Chicago: University of Chicago Press, 1958), pp. 222–28. Reprinted by permission of John Robert Moore and the University of Chicago Press.*

[1] For this quotation I am indebted to Mr. Godfrey Davies, who found it in an old notebook of Sir Charles Firth's.

"there is not an old woman that can go to the price of it, but buys thy *Life and Adventures*, and leaves it as a legacy, with *The Pilgrim's Progress, The Practice of Piety*, and *God's Revenge against Murther*, to her posterity." For *Robinson Crusoe* not only created a new literary form; it created a new reading public.

Because of its popularity among the semiliterate, there was a chance that it might sink to the level of the little chapbooks sold by itinerant peddlers. The Rev. James Woodforde purchased it with a life of a gypsy, *The Complete Fortune Teller*, and *Laugh and Grow Fat*, from "a traveling man and woman who sold all kinds of trifling books, &c." However, in 1806 the Rev. Mark Noble, hostile to Defoe as a Dissenter, admitted its almost universal acclaim: "I have never known but one person of sense who disliked it. Rousseau, and after him all France, applauded it." [2]

France was not alone in praising *Robinson Crusoe*. The story has shown the capacity to survive translation and sentimentalized adaptation and condensation and rewriting for children, preserving much of its potency in any garbled or truncated form. An Eskimo translation was published nearly a century ago in a newspaper in Greenland, illustrated with seven plates, one of which showed Friday prostrating himself before Crusoe to build a fire on the shore. Here, much as in the original, where the goatskins of Selkirk's cooler island were transferred to the tropics, we see Friday naked except for a scanty loincloth and Crusoe bundled tightly in furs as a true Eskimo, with a harpoon in the background and with waving palms and dense undergrowth on a low hill—the side of which is partly covered with snow. As in all great works of imagination, the inner vision has become more significant than external facts.

It has often been supposed that Crusoe was almost identical with Alexander Selkirk, but the influence of the Selkirk story on *Robinson Crusoe* has been greatly exaggerated. In all his writings Defoe had less to say about Selkirk's solitude in the Juan Fernández group west of Chile, on a real desert island 3,500 miles to the southwest of Crusoe's imaginary kingdom, than some other writers of the day. *A New Voyage Round the World* becomes more lively when Defoe's hero leaves the dull tasks of careening ship and catching goats on Selkirk's island to trade in Chile, and starts over the Andes on the exploration

[2] Joseph Spence, *Anecdotes* (London, 1820), pp. 258–59. Boswell's *Johnson* (Hill-Powell ed.; Oxford, 1934–50), III, 268, n. 1. Charles Gildon, *The Life and Strange Surprizing Adventures of Mr. D—— De F——, of London, Hosier* (London, 1719), pp. ix–x. *The Diary of a Country Parson*, ed. John Beresford (London, 1924–31), III, 353. The Rev. Mark Noble, *A Biographical History of England* (London, 1806), II, 306.

by which he hopes to prepare the way for his proposed English colony.
For Defoe at the beginning of 1719, the great fact was not that Selkirk
had returned to England seven years before but that in the new war
with Spain the South Sea Company's trade with Spanish America had
come to an abrupt end. He had long been interested in Sir Walter
Raleigh's attempts against Spain near the mouth of the Orinoco (where
Crusoe was to be shipwrecked), and by the end of 1719 he was urging
the South Sea Company, whose "charter begins at the River Oroono-
que," to develop the neighboring mainland of Guiana—the cannibal
coast from which the savages continued to endanger Crusoe on his
island: "the author of these sheets is ready to lay before them a plan
or chart of the rivers and shores, the depths of water, and all necessary
instructions for the navigation, with a scheme of the undertaking,
which he had the honor about thirty years ago to lay before King
William, and to demonstrate how easy it would be to bring the attempt
to perfection." [3] If the company declined this, he proposed that they
give leave to a society of merchants (perhaps including himself) to
undertake it for them.

Defoe had not yet established himself as the historian of the pirates.
But as a journalist he had already written of the increase of pirates in
the West Indies and of the appointment of Woodes Rogers in the
previous year as captain-general, governor, and vice-admiral of the
Bahama Islands to suppress them. If he wrote a novel in 1719, it would
likely have something to say of the slave trade, of the jealousy between
England and Spain, of pirates or mutineers (the rebellious sailors in
Robinson Crusoe never got further than mutineering), and of an island
near the mouth of the Orinoco River. No one could have foreseen how
Defoe would develop his hero's solitary life on the island. That was
apparently no part of his original plan for a narrative of wandering
travels, but came as a "strange surprise" to Defoe himself—perhaps the
most fortunate accident which ever befell any author in all literature.

Important as the public events of 1718 and early 1719 were for
Defoe, the roots of *Robinson Crusoe* lie deeper in his life. From childhood he had been a traveler, he had camped out in Surrey in a hut
as one of the boys who helped recover Sir Adam Brown's fish after
they had been scattered by a flood, he had baked tobacco pipes in his
kilns near Tilbury, he had long been interested in earthquakes. He
regarded swimming as an indispensable accomplishment, he had engaged in building boats and ships, his brothers-in-law were both ship-

[3] Nathan van Patten, "An Eskimo Translation of Defoe's 'Robinson Crusoe,'
Godthaab, Greenland, 1862–1865," *Papers of the Bibliographical Society of America*,
XXXVI (1942), 56–58. *An Historical Account of . . . Sir Walter Raleigh* (1719;
actually January, 1720), p. 55.

wrights, and when he wrote a historical account of the galleys of the ancients he sought advice from shipwrights about the possibility of operating three or four banks of oars. His own book on the Great Storm of 1703 was drawn on for Crusoe's two shipwrecks. His patron Sir Dalby Thomas had gone as governor of the African Company to the Guinea Coast, where Crusoe carried on his first commercial venture and toward which he was returning when he met with his great disaster. Defoe had a classmate at Morton's academy, Timothy Cruso or Crusoe, whose name (perhaps recalled by the island Curaçao [which Defoe spelled Curasoe] in the Caribbean) suggested the most famous name in all fiction. His early reading of Shakespeare suggested the method by which Governor Crusoe and his man Friday (like Prospero and Ariel in *The Tempest*) overcame their adversaries on the island.

It is possible that in failing to enter the ministry Defoe felt that he (like Crusoe) had disappointed his father. Certainly he gave his hero his own background as a Presbyterian who recalled the Shorter Westminster Catechism, read his Bible, and recorded his religious experience like any young Puritan. However skeptical we may be about interpreting the story as an allegory of Defoe's life, there are passages in which the memory of Defoe in Newgate certainly displaced the thought of Crusoe on his island: "How mercifully can our great Creator treat his creatures, even in those conditions in which they seem to be overwhelmed in destruction! How can he sweeten the bitterest providences, and give us cause to praise him for dungeons and prisons!" [4] It would be absurd to suppose that Defoe is identical with Crusoe; but no other author could have written this book.

In an article which Defoe wrote for Mist's *Weekly-Journal* of January 4, 1718, we find the hint for the otherwise incredible journey which Crusoe and Friday undertook from Lisbon to London in midwinter by way of the Pyrenees. Nothing would seem more unlikely than that the experienced traveler Crusoe would invite such unnecessary dangers and difficulties when he had returned so near to his home by the direct sea route. But in writing *Robinson Crusoe* a year later, Defoe could not resist the temptation to vary the adventures by using this earlier account of the danger of crossing the mountains in the snow, which he had ready at hand:

> Our letters from Roussillon and the countries bordering upon the Pyrenean Mountains give an account that the snows have already fallen there in prodigious quantities, and that the ravenous beasts of those

---

[4] Lee, I, title page and 32. *The History of the Principal Discoveries and Improvements* (1727), p. 32. Moore (28). Moore (29). Moore (11). *Robinson Crusoe* (Tegg ed.), I, 175.

countries begin to come down in great numbers into the forests and waste grounds on the side of Languedoc; that a troop of wolves, with six bears among them, came down into a village near—and attacked the inhabitants in the very market-place; that several were wounded by them. But we do not hear of any quite devoured, the people having taken arms, and assisting one another, attacked the cruel band of devourers, and killed fourteen of the wolves and two bears. Among the Wolves were some of a monstrous growth. The people of Languedoc have desired that one of the troops of hunters, established fifteen years ago by the King, may be allowed them, whose business it was, and for which they are paid equal to the horse of the Gens d'Arms, to hunt out and destroy wolves and other wild beasts. And we are told two troops will be ordered them, one into Languedoc and the other to Roussillon. And it is said the King of Spain has ordered six troops to be raised for the same purpose on the other side of the mountains, viz., in Catalonia, Arragon, and Navarre, where the same creatures make terrible havoc, and where a troop of wolves devoured five troopers, notwithstanding their firearms, and ate them all up, horses and all. . . .

It is unnecessary to point out more of these numerous analogues. Defoe knew human life through experience and observation, as well as through his wide reading; and he had the artist's supreme gift of assimilating everything for his creative purpose.

> A writer in *The Gentleman's Magazine* observes, "De Foe's life must itself have been singular. Whence came so able a geographer? Not only a geographer, but so well acquainted with the manners of savages, and with the productions, animal and vegetable, of America? Whence came he not only so knowing in trade, but so able a mechanic, and versed in so many trades? Admirably as Dr. Swift has contrived to conceive proportional ideas of giants and pigmies, and to form his calculations accordingly, he is superficial when compared with the details in *Robinson Crusoe*. The Doctor was an able satirist; De Foe might have founded a colony."

The last sentence suggests the profound difference between two great books. As one writer has stated it, Robinson Crusoe and Lemuel Gulliver "are unaccommodated man, poor, bare, and forked mankind stripped of its lendings. But the point is that Gulliver took off his clothes while Crusoe put them on."

The realism of *Robinson Crusoe* has been much admired, but perhaps overemphasized. It is true that some details to which objections have been raised—such as the northward drive of the Caribs (cannibals) across the continent of South America, their use of uninhabited Caribbean islands for occasional feasts on human flesh, and the dislike of the natives for salt—can be justified from sources familiar to Defoe.

John Robert Moore

M. Louis Rhead, who made a detailed study of the island which he mistakenly regarded as Defoe's original, decided that Defoe's information is "wonderfully true as far as it goes." A more recent writer has pitched his claim for Defoe's realism even higher and has hailed *Robinson Crusoe* as "exactly classical" because it is based on the classical law that one should be romantic in action but realistic in thought.[5]

The wanderings of Crusoe in the first two parts, even more the moral essays of the third part, could be equaled or surpassed elsewhere. It is in the island episode, in which Crusoe comes face to face with the problems of mankind, that we have the supreme achievement. It was here that Defoe must have been led to recall the experiences of Robert Knox on Ceylon and of Alexander Selkirk on one of the Juan Fernández islands; but the story as he tells it is far superior to any other. In the end, it is the imagination that counts most in *Robinson Crusoe*. Coleridge was right in stressing what he called "the *desert island* feeling"; nowhere in all literature before Defoe could one anticipate the cry of the Ancient Mariner,

> Alone, alone, all, all alone,
> Alone on a wide, wide sea!

And Coleridge was equally right in pointing out how much would have been lost if Defoe's hero had been given unusual abilities. For

then Crusoe would have ceased to be the universal representative, the person for whom every reader could substitute himself. But now nothing is done, thought, suffered, or desired, but what every man can imagine himself doing, thinking, feeling, or wishing for. Even so very easy a problem as that of finding a substitute for ink is with exquisite judgment made to baffle Crusoe's inventive faculties. And in what he does, he arrives at no excellence; he does not make basket work like Will Atkins; the carpentering, tailoring, pottery, &c., are all just what will answer his purposes, and those are confined to needs that all men have, and comforts that all men desire.

In modern life and modern literature, the Crusoe situation creeps in wherever man conquers his environment or adapts himself to adverse circumstances. When Sir Winston Churchill tells of his family life at Chartwell between two wars, we hear the familiar ring in the concrete details and sense the imaginative satisfaction that lies back

[5] Wilson (1), III, 444, n. F. W. D. Taylor, review of *Swift and Defoe: A Study in Relationship* by John F. Ross (*RES*, XIX [1943], 90). Louis Rhead, Introduction to *The Life and Strange Surprizing Adventures of Robinson Crusoe* (New York, 1900). "In Praise of Robinson Crusoe," *Athenaeum*, April 25, 1909, p. 230.

of their recapitulation. In the humble society of *The Wind in the Willows*, Mole seeks food in his abandoned home to entertain Rat; and once again we recognize the authentic tone of *Robinson Crusoe*: "The result was not so very depressing after all, though of course it might have been better; a tin of sardines—a box of captain's biscuits, nearly full—and a German sausage encased in silver paper." [6] When Ralph Edwards made his dugout canoe in the Canadian Rockies, all he knew about such boat-building "was what he recalled from reading *Robinson Crusoe*." More than 130 years ago, an early explorer in the African hinterland east of Timbuktu told of his solitude during the rainy season at Kouka:

> I had, indeed, already a little menagerie, which, if I would have allowed it, the sheikh would have added to daily, and I found in them great amusement—I might almost say much comfort. My collection consisted, besides my Loggun bird, of two monkeys, five parrots, a civet cat, a young ichneumon, and a still younger hyena: they had all become sociable with each other, and with me, and had their separate corners allotted them in the inclosure that surrounded my hut, except the parrots and the monkeys, who were at liberty; and while sitting in the midst of them of a morning, with my mess of rice and milk, I have often cast my thoughts to England, and reflected with deep interest on the singular chances of life by which I was placed in a situation so nearly resembling the adventurous hero of my youthful sympathies, Robinson Crusoe.

Amid all the changes that have taken place in South America and the neighboring islands of the Caribbean Sea, an island which has no location on modern maps still holds its own in the thoughts and affections of men:

> For whatsoever one hath well said goeth forth with a voice that never dieth.[7]

[6] S. T. Coleridge, *The Table Talk and Omniana*, ed. T. Ashe (London, 1884), p. 294. *The Literary Remains of Samuel Taylor Coleridge*, ed. Henry Nelson Coleridge (London, 1836), I, 197. Winston S. Churchill, *The Gathering Storm* (Boston, 1948), p. 79. Kenneth Grahame, *The Wind in the Willows* (New York, 1909), pp. 108–9.
[7] Leland Stowe, "The Amazing Crusoes of Lonesome Lake," *Reader's Digest* (February, 1957), p. 86. *Narrative of Travels and Discoveries in Northern and Central Africa, in the Years 1822, 1823, and 1824, by Major Denham, F.R.S., Captain Clipperton, and the Late Doctor Oudney* (2d ed.; London, 1826), I, 285. Pindar, "Fourth Isthmian Ode," trans. Sir John Sandys (*The Odes of Pindar* [Loeb ed.; London and New York, 1919], p. 465).

Defoe

by E. M. W. Tillyard

"Mr Jennings, do you happen to be acquainted with Robinson Crusoe?"

I answered that I had read Robinson Crusoe *when I was a child.*

"Not since then?" inquired Betteredge.

"Not since then."

"He has not read Robinson Crusoe *since he was a child,"* *said Betteredge, speaking to himself—not to me. "Let's try how* Robinson Crusoe *strikes him now!"*

(WILKIE COLLINS, *The Moonstone*)

(a) *Introductory*

In spite of its former great popularity, I doubt if *Robinson Crusoe*[1] was usually read aright. Robinson's lonely struggle with physical conditions on the island caught men's imaginations so powerfully that they failed to do justice to anything else and especially to the events which Defoe planned with such care in order to lead up to the culminating shipwreck. Thus the book was made simpler than it actually is, and was degraded from adult to adolescent reading. Today, superseded as the classic book for boys, it has lost its ill-grounded vogue. Of course, it has its readers, and of these a bigger proportion than for many years before may read it in the right way. Even so, it is read too little and prized too low.

From E. M. W. Tillyard, The Epic Strain in the English Novel *(Fair Lawn, New Jersey: Essential Books, 1958), pp. 31–50. Copyright © 1958 by E. M. W. Tillyard. Reprinted by permission of Oxford University Press, Inc. and Chatto & Windus Ltd.*

[1] I wish to record debts to: James Sutherland, *Defoe,* especially chap. XI; S. C. Sen, *Daniel De Foe, His Art and Mind* (Calcutta 1948); Edwin B. Benjamin, "Symbolic Elements in *Robinson Crusoe,*" in *Philological Quarterly,* 1951, pp. 206–11.

To Defoe's other novels, *Moll Flanders, Colonel Jacque,* and *Roxana,* modern readers do better justice than did their elders, but tend to make them Defoe's norm. By so doing they fail to see that as a work of art *Robinson Crusoe* is in a different and a higher category. It is constructed with a closeness that the other novels (rightly enough in view of their nature) do not attempt, and it touches greater depths of the mind.

It is hard to believe that Defoe was anything but an opportunist in his initial motions towards a piece of writing. He wrote immensely and as occasion presented or demanded. Excited by stories of seafarers surviving alone on uninhabited islands, he thought the theme might reach the hearts of others and that he might profit by writing it up. But his excitement went deeper than ever before or after (and probably deeper than he knew) and drove him to fasten on to his theme with unique intensity. In his other novels he could have added or removed incidents with no detriment to the whole: in *Robinson Crusoe* this is not so; even the removal of things which at first sight could be spared easily would in fact damage the total proportions. The notorious example of such a thing occurs near the end: the elaborate incident of Crusoe and his fellow-travellers from Lisbon being attacked by wolves in the Pyrenees. Now, in the middle, just before the great battle with the wolves as darkness falls Defoe lets us know through a sudden reference back to the book's beginning that he has his total impression in mind:

> The howling of wolves run much in my head; and indeed, except the noise I once heard on the shore of Africa, of which I have said something already, I never heard anything that filled me with so much horror.[2]

Crusoe heard these other dreadful animal noises when he was escaping from his Moorish captor in the boat with the shoulder-of-mutton sail. But then, as later when the wolves attacked, he was a free man, and he had a companion, the Moorish boy, Xury. Alone on the island, Robinson had no wild beasts to contend with: the arena was cleared for the struggle with himself. Freed from the island, he reverts to his old liability to the bestial foe. The Pyrenean wolves join with the African lions in framing Robinson's island-life, and they cannot be spared. They serve too to prevent Robinson's final return to the safety and the comforts of England from being too abrupt.

[2] P. 276.

(b) The Theme

If then an episode, usually thought superfluous, turns out to be indispensable, we should be the readier to expect the closest interlocking elsewhere.

To counteract the old habit of reading *Robinson Crusoe* merely for the sake of certain happenings on the island and to show that it is a richer and closer-knit work of art than Defoe's other narratives, I shall have to describe its plotting in some detail. In so doing I shall have in mind not only this closeness of construction but the richness of reference the plot contains, the amount of tradition which, consciously or unconsciously, it embodies. I shall in fact have my eye on the epic quality of variety as well as that of control.

You can describe the plot of *Robinson Crusoe* in several ways; and this possible multiplicity is one reason why the book holds us so strongly. You can begin by describing it as a version of the story of the Prodigal Son, references to which, either implied or stated, occur often in the opening pages. Robinson is the Prodigal who leaves his father's house against advice, who ruins himself not by riotous living but by a roaming disposition, who is left solitary and apparently desolate, who repents, and returns to his father (now in the form of God), and for whom God as it were kills the fatted calf, blessing him with abundance on the island and restoring him to favour and lordship. The climax of this succession comes before the dreadful sight of the footprint in the sand ruins Robinson's peace and enlarges the action's scope. It is marked by his exclamations:

> How mercifully can our great Creator treat his creatures, even in those conditions in which they seemed to be overwhelmed in destruction! How can he sweeten the bitterest providences and give us cause to praise him for dungeons and prisons! What a table was here spread for me in the wilderness, where I saw nothing at first but to perish for hunger! It would have made a stoic smile to have seen me and my little family sit down to dinner. There was my majesty, the prince and lord of the whole island; I had the lives of all my subjects at my absolute command. . . . Then to see how like a king I dined, too, all alone, attended by my servants.[3]

Or you can describe the book in terms not unlike the progression from Do-well through Do-bet to Do-best in *Piers Plowman*: the progression from the practical life to the life of contemplation in its turn fitting man for an existence where action and contemplation are

[3] Pp. 137–38.

combined. Crusoe, at first making a wreck of his life, rehabilitates himself on the island, beginning with his success in making the best practical job of his condition, then brought, through his solitude and his perils, face to face with God, and finally returning to society and meeting its problems in a way he could not do in his first state.

Or, most justly of all, you can describe the book in more abstract theological terms. Crusoe is Everyman, abounding in Original Sin, falling into specific folly and crime, incriminated more and more through repeated opportunities granted him by God for amendment, yet one of the Elect whom God has mysteriously reserved to be saved through chastisement.

These accounts of the theme of *Robinson Crusoe* should have brought out what is a great source of the book's strength: its large, if unconscious, debt to an old tradition. Just as the Puritan preachers were the heirs of the medieval preachers, so Defoe inherits a didactic or allegorical scheme rooted in the Middle Ages and modified by Puritan theology. And it is through applying these inherited things to the current mode of the realistic tale of unaristocratic life that Defoe creates so adorable an impression of freshness and rejuvenation. He combines the emotional appeals both of being the good old firm and of being under entirely new management.

(c) *The Development of the Theme*

I said above that most readers of *Robinson Crusoe* were so centred in the island and what happened there that they paid little heed to the rest. I had therefore better point out what is abundantly plain to any unprejudiced reader: that Defoe both leads up to the shipwreck on the island with solemn leisure and abundant motivation and throughout the book refers back to those preliminary events with an insistence and an accuracy that show he had the whole book in solution in his head throughout composition. The opening pages, describing Robinson's "propension of nature to rove" and his father's persuasions against indulging it, ending with the prophecy that, if he does, God will not bless him and that he will "have leisure hereafter to reflect upon having neglected his counsel when there might be none to assist in my recovery," state the theme. Robinson makes matters worse than they might have been by succumbing at once to the chance of a free passage from Hull to London and by failing to say a word to his parents about it or to ask God's blessing. Thus it was "in an ill hour, on the first of September, 1651, I went aboard a ship bound for London."

Defoe was too much of an artist and too vividly aware that God was slow to wrath to proceed at once to retribution. On the contrary, God both warns Crusoe and gives him repeated chances to mend his ways before confining him to his island prison. First, there is the storm off the Humber, in the terror of which his conscience reproaches him for "the breach of my duty to God and my father." But he cheers up and hardens his conscience when the weather mends. Then comes the great storm, the loss of the ship, and the safe landing of the crew near Yarmouth. And Defoe makes Crusoe say:

> Had I now had the sense to have gone back to Hull, and have gone home, I had been happy, and my father, an emblem of our blessed Saviour's parable, had even killed the fatted calf for me.[4]

Further, the captain of the boat warned Robinson that he was a predestinate Jonah and had no business to go to sea any more after God's visible warning. Unpersuaded, Crusoe goes to London by land. Again, God does not proceed at once to ruin him. He is fortunate in falling in with honest acquaintance in London and makes a successful voyage to Guinea and back, which brings him £300. Here was another good chance of reverting to the middle way of life at home. But Crusoe chooses a second voyage to the Guinea coast and undergoes his first chastisement in being captured by Moorish pirates and made the slave of a Moor of Sali on the coast of Morocco. But it is not an extreme chastisement. He is well treated and has company. Ultimately he escapes in a small boat with a Moorish boy and after sampling the terrors of beasts on the African coast is picked up by a Portuguese boat and taken to Brazil. As in London before, so on the Portuguese boat and in Brazil Crusoe falls in with honest acquaintance. He prospers as a planter. And yet he fails to learn the lessons both of his captivity and of his subsequent prosperity in the middle way of life. He decides he must get rich quicker and, needing more labour, joins with others in an illicit voyage to capture slaves: illicit, because the slave trade was a royal monopoly. This wanton abandonment of a settled life for a forbidden venture at last provokes God's anger, and Crusoe is thrown up, after shipwreck, on the desert island. Defoe links the preliminary adventures together by making Crusoe begin his last disastrous voyage on the same day of the year as his embarkation for his first voyage at Hull.

When Crusoe, after the shipwreck and his fight with the waves, at last "clambered up the cliffs of the shore and sat me down upon the grass, free from danger, and quite out of the reach of the water,"

---

[4] P. 11.

he instinctively thanked God for his extraordinary escape, showing that he was not altogether reprobate. But soon after, his fleeting and superficial gratitude gave way to a transport of despair; his regeneration will be a long process. During the night Crusoe's prospects are bettered through the ship's having been washed up near enough to the island to be accessible to a swimmer. He makes no mistake and takes every advantage of the profit offered him. After several journeys to and from the ship

> I had the biggest magazine of all kinds now that ever was laid up, I believe, for one man; but I was not satisfied still, for while the ship sat upright in that posture, I thought I ought to get everything out of her that I could.[5]

There is a beautiful irony in Crusoe's setting himself without delay to re-create in his desert that feeling for home and settlement which, as the very core of the middle way of life, he had abandoned and despised. Back from his last expedition to the ship before it broke up he writes:

> But I was gotten home to my little tent, where I lay with all my wealth about me very secure.

But not so secure really; and from acquisition Crusoe goes naturally on to make sure of what he has acquired. That done, he begins the long process of improving his lot through using the chances the island provides him; and with that process Defoe interweaves the other process of his spiritual rehabilitation. As Crusoe masters from the bare elements many of the attributes of civilised life, so he progresses from a bare instinct through reason to a faith in God. I doubt if Defoe consciously intended any symbolism, but unconsciously he was led to give Crusoe's culminating triumph in learning to grow corn, to make bread, and to bake pots for storing it some concurrent mental significance, to the incalculable benefit of his book. Anyhow, it was during Crusoe's highest inventive activity that through the earthquake and the fever God awakened his conscience and caused him to progress from the realm of reason to that of faith. Defoe manipulates this progress skilfully. He refers back to Crusoe's instinctive but fugitive religious feeling after being saved from the sea and he contrives that as Crusoe had several chances to lead a good life and rejected them, so he fails to act on several incipient motions of piety. And as those rejected chances led up to the shipwreck, so the neglected motions led up to the awful dream.

[5] P. 51.

As Crusoe comes to possess more of his mind, so he not only masters more techniques but he ranges farther afield in his island and takes a legitimate pride in being the master of it. But he has not altogether shed his old nature, and even after his regeneration he has wild thoughts of escape. These lead him to the folly of making a huge canoe he is unable to launch and of trying to circumnavigate the island in a small one. Barely escaping with his life, he accepts his reproof. He now governs his temper better, he has learnt to make his pots more efficiently, with a wheel, and he is shown (and this is the culmination of one part of the book) as the monarch of the island with his fortress home and his two plantations.

Thus Crusoe learnt to cope with solitude and with a life now devoid of violent turns and surprises. But that is a different matter from coping with society and its ways. And to that second aptitude he must be educated. It is this further education and the use to which Crusoe puts it that is the theme of the second half of the book. Defoe passes to this second half with perfect art. He does so, well before we are sated with the development of the first theme; and, just because we are not sated, we are open to the great stroke of surprise through which he makes the transition. This is the passage that follows immediately on the above account of Crusoe's solitary and sheltered prosperity:

> It happened one day, about noon, going towards my boat, I was exceedingly surprised with the print of a man's naked foot on the shore, which was very plain to be seen in the sand.[6]

The stark and yet somehow stealthy simplicity of this reminds me of another great stroke of the imagination, in Defoe's predecessor, Bunyan. In the *Holy War,* following directly on the ecstatic account of Mansoul's felicity after Emanuel has entered and reformed it, Bunyan introduces a sinister new character, marking a major turn in the story, with no more ado than

> But there was a man in the town of Mansoul, and his name was Mr Carnal Security; this man did, after all the mercy bestowed on the Corporation, bring the town of Mansoul into great and grievous slavery and bondage.

I speak roundly of Defoe's *art,* because the single footprint is poetic not literal truth; a probable impossibility, after Aristotle's fashion. Physically it was impossible that there should be but one footprint; artistically it is perfect that the vestige of society that Crusoe first encounters after his years of solitude should be minimal: the emphasis

[6] P. 142.

here will be in inverse proportion to the extent of the human manifestation. Even if Defoe had substituted no more than a detached foot, left over from one of the cannibal feasts, the effect, though more gruesome, would have been less profound; the very insubstantiality of the print awakens the imagination more and the reason less than any solid physical evidence would have done. Once aroused to the exclusion of reason, the imagination takes charge and pushes the horror to the extreme.

At first Crusoe seems in his terror to lose all the benefit of his preceding discipline. But he comes to accept the consequent profound change in his condition on the island, though never at ease in mind and ever prone to invading anxieties. Another great stroke of Defoe's art is that he waits before following up the footstep by more substantial ingressions of men. Crusoe resumes his work on the island; and the effect of the footstep is allowed to soften. It is only after a lapse of two years that he meets the remains of a cannibal feast. For two years more he has no other aim than to live close and escape notice. Then he grows bolder and considers action against the savages. More years elapse during which he learns to convert his first, instinctive, bloodthirsty thoughts of vengeance to the resolution, at once safer, more reasonable, and more pious, to leave vengeance to God and to abide the event. Having done so, he reaches a position of comparative stability. This slow timing is very remarkable in Defoe, who elsewhere tends to crowd his events thick, and it adds incalculably to the dignity of what happens on the island. It is as if the mood of reflection the island has come to signify is so profound that it must not be disturbed and abandoned too quickly. It must be partially prolonged into the period after the active life has begun. And there is great beauty in Crusoe's attaining this comparative stability of mind; for it recalls his previous more thorough but actually more precarious stability and at the same time, being comparative only, foretells future change.

That change occurs when the savages land, against custom, on Crusoe's side of the island, and when, soon after and against the reader's expectation, a new human element is introduced, the wreck off the island of a European ship. Nothing could be better than this ship's introduction just as our expectations are thoroughly concentrated on the savages. And nothing is more powerfully conceived in the whole book than Crusoe's yearning for human society, roused by the sight of the wreck:

> "Oh that it had been but one!" I believe I repeated the words, "Oh that it had been but one!" a thousand times; and the desires were so moved by it, that when I spoke the words my hands would clinch to-

gether, and my fingers press the palms of my hands, that if I had any
soft thing in my hand, it would have crushed it involuntarily; and my
teeth in my head would strike together and set against one another so
strong that for some time I could not part them again.[7]

And the incident is followed by the double irony of his finding the
"one" in the form of the dead boy washed up from the wreck, and
then, later, when he has given up hope and in the form he least
expected, the second "one" in the living man, Friday. There was no
sin in Crusoe's longing for a companion any more than there was in
Milton's Adam when he felt there was something lacking in Paradise
and God put things right by creating Eve. On the contrary, it was
now proper that Crusoe should be no longer content with the easi-
ness of his confined life. All the same he was wrong still to toy with
desperate plans of escape, yielding once more to his old sin of not
being satisfied with the station God had set him in and of embarking
on ill-considered ventures. He spent two years in this state, when God
intervened to help him. There is nothing finer in the book than the
account of Crusoe, in good health, unable for no apparent reason to
sleep, his mind and memory working with uncommon speed and
clarity, reviewing all his past life, marvelling at his blessed and prov-
idential security during the years before he saw the footprint and
truly grateful to God for it, but finally worked up into a feverish
desire to venture to sea on the slender hope of a rescue. Worn out he
fell asleep and had a dream, prophetic of later happening, of saving
a captive savage and of finding in him a companion and pilot in
escape. To this dream's direction he then turned his thoughts; but
God, slow to show his utmost favour as he had been slow to wrath,
keeps Crusoe waiting a year and a half before the prophecy is fulfilled and Friday becomes his slave.

Blessed by Friday's society, Crusoe acts virtuously in teaching him
the rudiments of Christianity and in so doing consolidates his own
faith. He has now served his penance and experiences real felicity. But
things do not quite follow the indications of the dream. Crusoe had
planned to go with Friday to join the Spaniards who, Friday told
him, were living with his own people; but a new landing of cannibals
interrupts the plan and leads to the rescue of Friday's father and a
Spaniard. There are now four on the island, and it is not for nothing
that Defoe reiterates the theme of kingship:

My island was now peopled, and I thought myself very rich in subjects;
and it was a merry reflection, which I frequently made, how like a king
I looked. First of all, the whole country was my own mere property, so

[7] Pp. 173–74.

that I had an undoubted right of dominion. Secondly, my people were perfectly subjected. I was absolute lord and lawgiver; they all owed their lives to me, and were ready to lay down their lives, if there had been occasion of it, for me. It was remarkable, too, we had but three subjects, and they were of three different religions. My man Friday was a Protestant, his father was a Pagan and a cannibal, and the Spaniard was a Papist. However, I allowed liberty of conscience throughout my dominions.[8]

This is, of course, "a merry reflection"; and aptly so, because we are beginning to get back to the world of men. But it is more: it marks a point in Crusoe's mental growth. He has reached a higher stature than when he was a king among his animal dependents, about to be thrown into confusion by the sight of the footprint. Nor should we overlook the mention of property. According to the kind of Protestantism with which Defoe was familiar, it was right that a good state of mind should receive a material reward.

Hereafter the action moves quicker. Crusoe acts wisely and humanely when the ship arrives and the mutineers land. His pretence of his being His Excellency the Governor with a bodyguard of fifty men both serves the plot and intensifies the idea of kingship. It has a tinge of comedy like the passage just quoted and yet it connotes a still greater mental stature in Crusoe. Having defeated the plans of the mutineers, he obtains a passage for himself and Friday on the ship and provides for the settlement of the island. When he returns to Europe he acts justly to the Portuguese captain and the English widow who had helped him, and disposes wisely of the wealth God had blessed him with. He ends having learnt his lesson and at peace with the middle way of life.

(d) *Suggestiveness*

I do not assert that the fullness and good order of the plot of *Robinson Crusoe* imply a great deal by themselves. It is when we add them to the other literary qualities Defoe commanded that we can estimate their full weight. They imply an intensity in the way he apprehended his story, a steady seriousness, unique in his novels.

Defoe may, as I have pleaded, conduct his story with great art. But it is, for all that, a simple story with few characters and no great diversity of events. Only through making these simplicities pregnant could he achieve the richness of content necessary for the epic effect. And that was precisely what he was able to do. None of the characters

[8] P. 227.

strikes our imagination powerfully except Crusoe himself; and he
is so limited (you have only to think of Hamlet to admit this) that
you wonder why he so impresses. But impress he does; and in two
quite different ways. James Sutherland was right in saying that
Crusoe "is first of all an Englishman of the lower middle classes
making the best of things"; and Coleridge[9] was also right in saying
that Defoe's excellence was "to make me forget my specific class,
character and circumstances and to raise me, while I read him, into
the universal man." And the reader feels like that because Crusoe
himself becomes universal man. Further, even in his first, narrower,
capacity Crusoe embraces both the elements, the adventurous and the
domestic, of contemporary puritanism. At the beginning he is dominated by the first, but this does not mean that the second is not there
underneath. On the contrary, the moment unmitigated adventure has
reached its logical, disastrous, end, all Crusoe's energy is turned to
making a home for himself, and out of seemingly intractable materials.
Defoe stages his union of the two elements with consummate skill. He
could, of course, have embodied them in two characters, one bred
to seafaring adventure, the other to trade at home, and allowed them
to live the lives to which their breeding pointed. Instead, he uses a
single character and makes him interesting through his contrariness
and pugnacity. Crusoe chooses adventure and chance when it was
easy for him to be mercantile and domestic; he fights for domestic
security when it was easier for him to fall into a despairing inertia and
to accept whatever chance or adventure put in his way. He thus
satisfies the two human instincts of being for and against the government. More narrowly he disinfects of their deadliness the deadly virtues of industry, thrift, sobriety, and punctuality. Over and above all
this, Crusoe in the great crises ceases to embody the great qualities of
contemporary puritanism and becomes the type of man himself in his
struggle with circumstance. No character in eighteenth-century fiction
embraces so much as Robinson Crusoe.

    This richness of the protagonist's character is matched constantly
by the rich suggestiveness of the incidents. All recognise Defoe's
special gift of making the reader believe, through the utter confidence
with which he goes into details, in the facts he presents. Most writers
are content that the reader should suspend willingly his disbelief;
Defoe is different in sometimes compelling the reader a little in the
direction of positive belief in the happening. Defoe's method in itself
is no better than the usual one; indeed it would stale quickly if
widely affected. But it suited Defoe and gave him his special flavour.
Now, in *Robinson Crusoe,* as nowhere else, Defoe used his special

---

[9] *Literary Remains* (London, 1836), i, p. 189.

kind of verisimilitude to achieve a rare emotional intensity. His epitaph on his comrades who perished in the shipwreck from which only he was saved is:

> I never saw them afterwards, or any sign of them, except three of their hats, one cap, and two shoes that were not fellows.[10]

It is, of course, the last detail that compels Defoe's peculiar kind of credibility. But it does more. It brings home the commonplace of the insensitiveness and disorderliness of mere nature (the sea couldn't even bother to wash up a *pair* of shoes); and it renders that heightened state of the human mind, when it not only experiences momentous feelings or makes wide general decisions but simultaneously notices the most trivial details. And, in so rendering, it stirs the mind of the reader to a state of uncommon receptiveness.

Defoe's observation of the two shoes' disparity is one of many such in *Robinson Crusoe,* and these, as well as having their immediate emotional effect, combine in making us see events through the eyes of the narrator. We tell ourselves not merely that these happenings are singularly lifelike but that Crusoe was an exceptionally observant man; so much so that we surrender ourselves willingly to see things through his eyes. In other words, we have the least possible sense of the author's presence and personal opinions, and a correspondingly strong dramatic sense of events happening to the narrator or seen through his eyes.

This general remark on *Robinson Crusoe* was provoked by a sentence that commemorated pitifully Crusoe's lost companions. Take now a passage in a different mood to illustrate the richness of art still further. It describes Crusoe's return to the island after his second expedition to the wreck:

> I was under some apprehensions during my absence from the land, that at least my provisions might be devoured on shore; but when I came back, I found no sign of any visitor, only there sat a creature like a wild cat upon one of the chests, which, when I came towards it, ran away a little distance, and then stood still. She sat very composed and unconcerned, and looked full in my face, as if she had a mind to be acquainted with me. I presented my gun at her; but as she did not understand it, she was perfectly unconcerned at it, nor did she offer to stir away; upon which I tossed her a bit of biscuit, though, by the way, I was not very free of it, for my store was not great. However, I spared her a bit, I say, and she went to it, smelled of it, and ate it, and looked (as pleased) for more; but I thanked her, and could spare no more, so she marched off.[11]

[10] P. 43.
[11] Pp. 50–51.

Such a passage is profoundly puzzling. How, one asks, did Defoe reach such perfection of description? how did he crowd much into a minute space through so simple and direct means? Did he picture the incident with so precise a vision that he wrote his words without a pause? or did he study his effects, for "effects" there are? For instance, he gives the effect of anxiety by using the word *devoured* and not *eaten:* the loss of his stores would be a disaster, to which the stronger word is appropriate. Again, *tossing* denotes a more leisurely action than throwing and corresponds to Crusoe's mood of idleness and amusement. No poet has made sound echo sense in a more masterly way than Defoe when he wrote "ran away a little distance, and then stood still." And near the end *smelled of it,* with its suggestion of a slower caution, fits the nature of cat better than the more abrupt *smelt it* would have done. And, in general, who has conveyed the essentials of cat-behaviour in so short a space: with such economy of means and with so much implied? He does not tell us, for instance, that the cat held her tail erect when she left, but the abrupt stiff rhythm of the last words forces that picture on us. The whole little account takes us by surprise; we feel, as we read it, like a very small boy who has lighted on a newly minted half-crown. But, for all the surprise, it has its own organic justification. The cat, though technically wild, behaves like a tame one—had Crusoe spared more biscuit he might have kept her—so that she reinforces the domestic theme which Defoe introduces as soon as the opposite theme has reached its logical end in disaster. The passage also makes credible or softens the absence of wild beasts on the island. Some wild life there must be, or we should be incredulous; but violent and dangerous beasts, such as Crusoe encountered before on the African coast and after in the Pyrenees, were out of place. Such skill in both setting off the passage by surprise and bringing it in so pat to forward the action or make credible the situation is as puzzling as the nature of the passage itself. This has the air of pondered and deliberate art; and yet such art is the last thing we expect of Defoe. However, the puzzlement is secondary. What matters is that the passage illustrates both the richness of content and the constructional skill that Defoe commanded in *Robinson Crusoe.*

(e) *Allegory*

As soon as we assert (or admit) that Crusoe is something more than the chief figure in a lively narrative, being the type both of the merchant adventurer of his own day and of mankind itself in certain difficulties, we have to decide whether to push such multiple significances farther. Present fashion tempts us to push them much farther, and my own temperament may be too ready to acquiesce in it. Making what allowance I can for these two factors, I cannot escape the conclusion that *Robinson Crusoe* is nearer to the sort of thing you get in Bunyan before and Kafka after than are any other of the chief novels of the eighteenth century. Tom Jones is a satisfactory comic hero, but in no way mankind; Mrs. Shandy cannot be bettered as a recognisable female character in a book of a certain kind, but has not begun to be Mother Eve simultaneously; and (extend the eighteenth-century mode into the next age) Jane Austen's young women have no other dimension than that of the dramatic fiction in which they exist. Crusoe is nearer to Milton's Adam and to Bunyan's Christian than to any of these. Nor is it surprising in view of Defoe's familiarity with the works of his Puritan predecessors. We can therefore expect some kind of multiple meaning not only in the protagonist but in some of the events of *Robinson Crusoe.*

The question is: in which? Edwin Benjamin goes so far as to see symbolic meanings in the two sides of the island and in the shoots of green barley that spring from the fortuitously scattered grain. The lush side of the island with its grapes, its turtles, and its steamier climate is said to stand for the luxurious temperament. Crusoe rightly decides to remain on the less lush and austerer side, which has its corresponding moral significance. The shoots of barley are also the shoots of grace newly sprung in Crusoe's heart. I do not believe in such precise and detailed symbolism, which could hardly exist without the author's conscious intention. On the other hand I agree (as I conveyed in describing the plot) with Benjamin's more general theory of a connection between Crusoe's victory over nature and his victory over himself. Because he progressively mastered himself he had the strength to master nature; and some of his physical victories are at the same time symbols of mental triumph. But, again, which? There is enormous force in Defoe's account of Crusoe making his pots. Should we see here the biblical allegory of God the potter and man the pot? is Crusoe's success in making the pot his own success, through God's help, in re-making himself? Again, I am reluctant to admit anything so worked out, so precise. And if Crusoe's potting is anywhere symbolic it is later, when, just after saying that his thoughts were "very much composed as to my condition and fully comforted in resigning myself to the dispositions of Providence," he says that he arrived at unexpected perfection in his earthenware, having learnt to use a wheel.[12] There may well be some correspondence here between

[12] P. 133.

the good order of Crusoe's thoughts and the regular motion of the potter's wheel. But as for the first, difficult, triumph in pot-making, it should not be separated from the larger process of making and storing bread. Of that process it is the most difficult and perhaps the culminating part, but it is subordinate to the whole. On the other hand I cannot confine the meaning of the total process of making and storing bread to the mere acts that are necessary to it. Bread is here the token of the civilised life and of the pure essentials not the trimmings of that life; and when Crusoe has learnt to grow the grain, to make the bread, and to store it he has made good as he could not have done through any other act.

This symbolic act of making bread unites with other things in the book to take the action out of its own day and to extend it back in time. On firing his first shot on the island, Crusoe's thoughts fly backward, for he comments: "I believe it was the first gun that had been fired there since the creation of the world." That is a homely way of putting it, and yet the sentiment is the romantically imaginative one of Tennyson's

> wind, that shrills
> All night in a waste land, where no one comes
> Or hath come, since the making of the world.

It is because Defoe commands this kind of imagination that his Crusoe represents both the middle-class pioneer of his own day and earlier man painfully inventing the arts of civilisation.

All in all, the precise limits of Defoe's symbolism do not matter much, if some sense of proportion is preserved. What does matter to the highest degree is that Defoe creates in a careful and unprejudiced reader that sharpened state of mind that knows it must be ready for the unusual and the richly significant.

What I have written so far has been meant to demonstrate among other things that the literary kind to which Defoe tends is the epic rather than tragedy, comedy, melodrama, satire, and so forth. He voices the "accepted unconscious metaphysic" of a large group of men and he qualifies as their spokesman by revealing a much more capacious mind than they themselves possess. But tending and arriving are different: and in the end I have to face the matter of Defoe's general quality of writing, for on that quality will depend his position on the road between setting forth and arriving.

It must be admitted first that the quality of style in *Robinson Crusoe* is not constant. Here, for instance, is a very poor piece of writing:

While we were in this condition, the men yet labouring at the oar to bring the boat near the shore, we could see when, our boat mounting the waves, we were able to see the shore, a great many people running along the shore to assist us when we should come near. But we made but slow way towards the shore, nor were able to reach the shore till, being past the lighthouse at Winterton, the shore falls off to the westward towards Cromer, and so the land broke off a little the violence of the wind. Here we got in, and, though not without much difficulty, got all safe on shore.[13]

Here the repetitions of the word *shore* could have been avoided with a little care and are very ugly. But such lapses are rare; and in general Defoe slides easily back and forth from full and expressive simplicity to high eloquence or great intensity. . . .

Defoe's qualities of writing are, indeed, great; but we must recognise his limitations. I first mentioned Pope along with Defoe, because Pope's *Iliad* and *Robinson Crusoe* belong to the same years; and I remarked how different were the two societies that the two authors span. It comes as a shock to reflect that Pope was the younger man by a whole generation, so that it is hardly fair to use one of the two to illustrate the deficiency of the other. It comes as an equal shock to reflect that Congreve, whom we associate with Restoration drama, was nine years *younger* than Defoe, whom we associate with the eighteenth-century novel. But we shall be justified in using Congreve rather than Pope as the measure of what Defoe could not compass. The matter presents itself to me best in terms of flexibility and rigidity. It is not that Defoe had a rigid mind. On the contrary, Sutherland is right in speaking of his puckish spirit in his satire, the *Consolidator*:

Defoe was the awkward boy who will persist in asking questions; the difference is that he knew quite well that he was being awkward . . . A bourgeois who delights to *épater les bourgeois*.[14]

Nevertheless, Defoe cannot overcome the rigidity of his given material. If he is to remain true to his choric task (a task of course not consciously conceived as such) of voicing the dissenting habit of mind, he cannot be too critical, he must identify himself with it. And the type of religion in question with its simple elections, interventions, rewards, admonitions, and punishments, and the type of mercantile morality in question with its surface justice and its ruthless self-seeking, could not be made flexible by however sensitive and imaginative an observer. Congreve's Mirabel and Millamant, with their affec-

[13] Pp. 10–11.
[14] *Defoe*, p. 143.

tations of frivolity and heartlessness advanced to screen much seriousness and warmth of feeling, betoken a world where mind can move with
greater freedom, between more distant extremes. Defoe has his advantages. He can oscillate between present and past, between actual
contemporary people and mankind in abstraction or mankind in a
primitive phase of culture; but within his own contemporary province
his oscillations are a good deal more confined. The styles of the two
authors, so well attuned to their substance, confirm the contrast.
Defoe's simplicity can compass the homeliness of the day and the
timelessness of abstracted human nature but it lacks the subtle
elegance, the diversified tempo, and the overtones and undertones of
Congreve. This comparison is not a complaint that Defoe was not
other than he was; it merely attempts to point out that however much
we like Defoe and feel enthusiastically about him we must avoid
the temptation of inflating his genius. I believe *Robinson Crusoe*
to be an epic, but an epic having some of the limitations of the middle-
class ethos whose choric expression it was.

Religion and Invention in *Robinson Crusoe*

by *William H. Halewood*

I

In a piece which is in some ways the *Shamela* of Defoe commentary, Charles Gildon's "The Life and Strange Surprizing Adventures of Mr. D[aniel] De F[oe]," Robinson Crusoe is made to upbraid his creator for falsifying his story. "All this," he declares at one point, "came out of thy inventive noddle." The charge has seldom been repeated, and although there are increasing signs of a disposition to give Defoe his due as a novelist of imagination, critics who make claims for his inventiveness of noddle have still to make way against the notion that his imagination was bound by the facts of his personal experience and that his characters are simply himself got up in an assortment of easily penetrated disguises. There is evidence to be brought against this view in the slighted passages in *Robinson Crusoe* which treat Crusoe's spiritual crises. For Crusoe has the crises of a mystic, and while it is plainly untrue that Defoe himself lacked all religion (another suggestion of Gildon's, which has shown greater staying power), one can scarcely conceive of his sharing Crusoe's mystical intensities. Behind Crusoe's warmth, as I shall try to show, is a cool-headed Defoe intent upon his novelist's work.

Crusoe's warmest and most characteristic emotion, his anxiety for his soul, is first fully glimpsed in the vivid account of his "vision" early in his stay on the island.

> I thought that I was sitting on the ground, on the outside of my wall, where I sat when the storm blew after the earthquake, and that I saw a man descend from a great black cloud, in a bright flame of fire, and light upon the ground. He was all over as bright as a flame, so that I could but just bear to look towards him. His countenance was most inexpressibly dreadful, impossible for words to describe. When

William H. Halewood, "Religion and Invention in Robinson Crusoe," Essays in Criticism, *XIV (October 1964), 339–51. Reprinted by permission of F. W. Bateson, editor of* Essays in Criticism.

he stepped upon the ground with his feet I thought the earth trembled, just as it had done before in the earthquake, and all the air looked, to my apprehension, as if it had been filled with flashes of fire.

He was no sooner landed upon earth but he moved forwards toward me, with a long spear or weapon in his hand, to kill me; and when he came to a rising ground at some distance, he spoke to me, or I heard a voice so terrible that it is impossible to express the terror of it. All that I can say I understood was this: "Seeing all these things have not brought thee to repentance, now thou shalt die"; at which words I thought he lifted up the spear that was in his hand to kill me.[1]

That the figure "steps upon the ground *with his feet*," may perhaps be taken as an instance of the kind of imagining which Defoe's critics have always recognized, the imagining of unnecessary physical detail by the "greatest liar that ever lived" in order to give his tale the appearance of *bona fide* narrative. But surely as remarkable in the rendering of the vision is the imagination which *excludes* physical detail, even such detail as might seem necessary to set the scene fully before us. The countenance of the man is "most inexpressibly dreadful, impossible for words to describe," and his voice, or a voice apparently his, is so terrible that "it is impossible to express the terror of it." What Defoe achieves by omitting description of the face and voice of the visitor from heaven, or hell, is not merely a sense of the mental agitation and confusion of his hero, although that in itself is no mean feat of narration, but he also, and more remarkably, imagines an experience to which human senses are not equal (and to which, if his imagination were as sense-bound as most of his critics have insisted, Defoe as a novelist would not be equal); and he shows an awareness of the limitations of his art, a novelistic tact, in avoiding sensuous description and giving us the vision in terms which enhance its vagueness and awesomeness.

Crusoe has only one such moment of transport, but moments of intense spiritual consciousness are frequent in his story and are given significant emphasis. They are the moments in which his emotion is most strongly concentrated and which in turn evoke the strongest emotional responses from the reader. Indeed, it can hardly be correct that, as Ian Watt has said in *The Rise of the Novel* (Berkeley, 1958, p. 76), "The modern reader . . . tends to pay little attention to these parts of the narrative." Few other parts of the narrative make so insistent a demand for his attention, and were they lacking, one suspects, it would not be read at all. Even the extended passages of "reflection" in *Robinson Crusoe,* the pious

[1] *The Life and Strange Surprizing Adventures of Robinson Crusoe,* ed. G. H. Maynadier (New York, 1905), p. 97.

ruminations of the hero which come without the stimulation of crisis, demand attention as foci of emotion. The report of Crusoe's spiritual progress to the fourth anniversary of his arrival on the island is a case in point. We are told that in the four years "by a constant study and serious application of the Word of God and by assistance of His grace" Crusoe has gained a new view of his situation. He is able now to regard the world as well-lost and to find advantages, mundane as well as spiritual, in his island life. He is led to consider his past errors—his disregard of his father's instructions and remonstrances, his seafaring, his failure to pray or even to say "Thank God" for his various deliverances—and to hope "that God had yet mercy in store" for him. To be sure, these reflections open no new vistas on the human spirit. They are no more than we might expect from the character described by Coleridge as "the universal representative, the person for whom every reader could substitute himself." [2] But they serve to give us a sense of the meaning of Crusoe's experience to himself such as we expect heroes of novels to give us; they convey his emotions of hope, anxiety, and regret; and they take us into his mind as do no other passages in the novel, illuminating his character and motives and making his behaviour intelligible.

They have a further usefulness, as can be seen in the instance just cited, in that by recapitulating earlier action and anticipating later, involving time past and time future in time present, they give a more substantial unity and coherence to the narrative while complicating its simple consecutive movement. And they help to unify the story by their mere continuousness. For with the exception of his planting and harvesting, themselves occasions of reflection ("I ought to consider that I was fed even by miracle, even as great as that of feeding Elijah by ravens; nay by a long series of miracles . . ."), none of Crusoe's other occupations are regularly recurrent, and the accounts of most can be read as completely detachable episodes. Thus at the conclusion of his almost disastrous attempt to sail his boat around the island he thanks God and goes to sleep, and the incident, which occupied a day, is closed (p. 158). His religious reflections on the other hand are unceasing, and we are reminded that they go on even when the narrative is concerned with other matters: "These thoughts took me up many hours, days, nay, I may say, weeks and months" (p. 176), or, again, "I had terrible reflections upon my mind for many months" (p. 147). Indeed, the reflective mood is felt throughout the book. It is not introduced anew, but merely brought into prominence on those occasions when Crusoe simply sits and thinks, or when reflection

[2] S. T. Coleridge, *Miscellanies, Aesthetic and Literary,* ed. T. Ashe (London, 1892), p. 160.

attends climactic incident. Thus we are not unprepared for his sur-
mise that the footprint he has found on the shore is the Devil's. He
has been reflecting for years that "Nothing happens without God's
appointment," that "He has appointed all this to befall me" (p. 103),
and that, given all his wickedness, there is something marvellous in
the fact that he was not "long ago destroyed" (p. 103). It is religious
reflection then which makes the incidents, both internal and external,
emotionally consistent, and which, in fact, establishes the consistency
and continuity of Crusoe's character. Indeed, it provides him with
a characteristic vocabulary, a Bunyan-like language of reflection which
he uses even when his mind is otherwise employed (e.g., "I began
sorely to repent that I had dug my cave so large . . .").

II

Watt has said that otherworldly concerns "punctuate Defoe's novels
with comminatory codas" (p. 81), a view which perhaps does justice
to the pious reflections of all of Defoe's heroes and heroines with the
exception of Crusoe. In Crusoe's story, however, the reflections are
not codas, but climaxes. His greatest adventure is his spiritual one, and
this can be seen, from one point of view, as a matter of novelistic
necessity. Crusoe's soul comes into prominence as other possible sources
of interest recede: in his perfect isolation he must enter into a dialogue
with his soul or enter into no dialogue at all. Certain of the passages
of reflection are, of course, more climactic than others, but all treat
critical junctures in Crusoe's inner experience; indeed, all are episodes
in the "Puritan drama of the soul," the spiritual agon of the Christian
left alone to discover whether he is to be saved or damned. To be so
situated, it has been said, gives "an heroic proportion and a tragic
mode to the experience of the individual." [3] And it is when this
situation is represented in its most harrowing simplicity, not tangled
with the details of his daily life, that Crusoe most engages us as a
hero and that his narrative seems most to justify our attention.

A rather lengthy passage of this kind occurs shortly after the account of the vision. Crusoe is in the process of "conversion," still
not fully possessed of "a sense of his condition," which he comes to
by somewhat clumsy steps.

> As I sat there, some such thoughts as these occurred to me.
> What is this earth and sea of which I have seen so much? Whence

[3] Allen Tate, "Emily Dickinson," *The Man of Letters in the Modern World* (New
York, 1955), p. 213.

is it produced? And what am I, and all the other creatures, wild and tame, human and brutal, whence are we? Sure we are all made by some secret Power, who formed the earth and sea, the air and sky. And who is that?

Then it followed most naturally, It is God that has made it all. Well, but then it came on strangely, if God has made all these things, He guides and governs them all, and all things that concern them; for the power that could make all things, must certainly have power to guide and direct them.

If so, nothing can happen in the great circuit of His works, either without His knowledge or appointment. And if nothing happens without His knowledge, He knows that I am here, and am in this dreadful condition. And if nothing happens without His appointment, He has appointed all this to befall me.

Nothing occurred to my thoughts to contradict any of these conclusions; and therefore it rested upon me with the greater force, that I was brought to this miserable circumstance by His direction. He having the sole power, not of me only, but of everything that happened in the world. Immediately it followed, Why has God done this to me: What have I done to be thus used?

My conscience presently checked me in that inquiry, as if I had blasphemed, and methought it spoke to me like a voice: "Wretch! dost thou ask what thou has done? Look back upon a dreadful, misspent life, and ask thyself what thou has done? Ask, why is it that thou wert not long ago destroyed? Why wert thou not drowned in Yarmouth Roads; killed in the fight when the ship was taken by the Sallee man-of-war; devoured by the wild beasts on the coast of Africa; or drowned here, when all the crew perished but thyself? Dost thou ask, What have I done?"

I was struck dumb with these reflections, as one astonished, and not a word to say . . . (pp. 102–3).

The fumbling questions with which reflection begins, ostensibly the catechizings of an unpracticed intelligence, are not very convincingly represented, and the reader may be excused if he does not take them seriously. But they are plainly calculated to dramatize Crusoe's dilemma; and if Defoe has failed to achieve drama, it is clear, nonetheless, that he knows where the dramatic possibilities in his story lie and has sought to exploit them. And as the passage develops he is more successful. The questions and answers lose their abstract and objective quality as Crusoe comes more strongly into a sense of the encirclements of a "Power" bent on bringing him to misery, and with the final swift transition from self-pity to self-condemnation we are made to feel the shock of a tragic reversal in the drama of Puritan introspection.

Not the least remarkable feature of that drama as Defoe represents it is the hero's extraordinary self-consciousness; for Crusoe keeps as anxious a watch over his reflections as he does over the landings of the savages, and is as quick to take alarm from them. On one occasion, when he has opened his Bible to the words "I will never, never leave thee, nor forsake thee," he is led to reflect that the assurance of the "the favor and blessing of God" infinitely outweighs the inconveniences of being forsaken by men, and he comes to the point of "giving thanks to God for bringing me to this place." He immediately detects the falseness of the impulse, however. "I know not what it was, but something shocked my mind at that thought and I durst not speak the words. 'How canst thou be such a hypocrite,' said I, even audibly, 'to pretend to be thankful for a condition which, however thou mayest endeavour to be contented with, thou wouldst rather pray heartily to be delivered from?' So I stopped there . . ." (p. 127).

Crusoe is never, to be sure, the victim of his impulses. He is circumspect—indeed, fussily analytical—in his approach to every problem, and such mental habits have much to do with his success in escaping from Sallee, in establishing his plantation in Brazil and, in the central part of the book, in making himself "the master of every mechanic art." But it is plainly a more complex and more exciting kind of analysis that is involved in the passages of reflection. Its subject— the hero's soul, its present condition and the prospect of its welfare in eternity—is, as Defoe makes clear, of infinitely greater moment; and the process, owing to the fact that the soul has its own principles of motion, is one of greater subtlety and difficulty. It gives us what I have said are the climaxes of the story, the moments of exalted consciousness and high emotion when the processes of analysis and criticism are themselves analysed and criticized, often with results that leave Crusoe's mind "shocked."

III

It is necessary, to be sure, to speak of "climaxes" in the plural in *Robinson Crusoe*, for its structure is paratactic. There is no single point to which rising action rises and from which falling action falls. And in so far as the climaxes are climaxes in Crusoe's religious life, the paratactic structure reflects the inconclusiveness of his religious experiences. None results in his permanent regeneration, and none, as critics from Gildon to Watt have deplored, has a significant effect on his practical activity. There is, as Watt has said, a "discontinuity between the religious aspects of the book and its action" (p. 81)—or, at least, between the religious concerns of the hero and *his* actions. But it seems mistaken to conclude, as critics have, that this reflects the inadequacy of Defoe's own religious conceptions; for there is abundant evidence in the novel that Defoe was aware of the shortcomings of Crusoe's religion. Crusoe himself, for example, repeatedly calls attention to the fact that its effects are not lasting and its control over his thoughts and actions not dependable. Thus he reports the dwindling of his religious awe after the earthquake which occurred early in his stay on the island: "No sooner was the first fright over, but the impression it made went off also. I had no more sense of God or his judgments, much less of the present affliction of my circumstances being from His hand, than if I had been in the most prosperous condition of life" (p. 100). The discovery of the footprint leads also to the discovery that fear had "banished all my religious hope" (p. 174). And later, preoccupied with his plan of escaping to the mainland, he again loses, and marks the loss, of the benefit of his reflections: "All my calm of mind, in my resignation to Providence, and waiting the issue of the depositions of Heaven seemed to be suspended . . ." (pp. 222–23).

Surely it is clear that Defoe knew Crusoe's religion to be imperfect and that he deliberately made it so. In fact, the imperfections of Crusoe's religion can be explained by the same necessity that I have cited as explaining the peculiar prominence of religion in the novel —the necessity of finding a substitute for human beings and for the interest of human relationships and human conflict. For more familiar kinds of conflict, I have argued, Defoe substitutes the "Puritan drama of the soul," and this he seeks to intensify by making Crusoe's reach exceed his grasp. Crusoe never conquers; the "master of every mechanic art" and of his island is not equally the master of his inner life, which repeatedly tricks and surprises him.

Crusoe's religious soul, in fact, becomes his antagonist. It is objectified, almost as a character, provided with an independent point of view, a voice, and lines to speak. Except for Crusoe himself and the usually silent parrot, it provides the only speech in the central part of the novel. Moreover, it alone succeeds in provoking Crusoe to speech—with the result that the passages of reflection in *Robinson Crusoe* are the only passages of dialogue. How spirited a dialogue excerpts already quoted have shown:

"Wretch dost thou ask what thou hast done?"

"How can thou be such an hypocrite?"

"Jesus, Thou son of David! Jesus, Thou exalted Prince
   and Saviour, give me repentance!"

That Defoe's employment of the soul as antagonist and interlocutor is deliberate and calculated can hardly, I think, be questioned:
it is too efficient, too fully exploited, to be merely a random benefit
of his own experience of Puritan spirituality. As an antagonist which
neither conquers nor is conquered the soul provokes crises which
must always be repeated, giving the tale something of the character
of a prolonged and heated psychomachy and a structure of continuous
episodes. As interlocutor it provides talk—as beneficial to the novel
as to its hero. Crusoe, indeed, suggests its necessity: "When I began
to regret the want of conversation, I would ask myself whether this
conversing mutually with my own thoughts and, as I hope I may
say, with even God himself, by ejaculations, was not better than the
utmost enjoyment of human society in the world?" (p. 152). The
answer of Defoe's reader, I think, must be that it is at least as good.

In summary then, it may be said that the "discontinuity between
religion and action" in *Robinson Crusoe,* the failure of Crusoe to
achieve the full and final illumination which would transform his
practical behaviour, is made to serve the ends of the novelist's art in
things both great and small. It gives the book its structure, justifies
its length and method, contributes to its air of authenticity, provides
emotional complexity and depth, and enlivens its language. Surely
we may conclude that Crusoe's chronic lapsing is a planned part of the
story.

IV

All of Crusoe's lapses, of course, are not conscious ones, and his
struggles with his soul do not all have an heroic proportion. As a
"universal representative" he is essentially a naïve hero; and, although
he has the habit of self-scrutiny, his inward vision is not unclouded.
Thus critics who have deplored his failure even to understand his religion are partially justified by the fact that the discontinuity between
his religious attitudes and his practical behaviour is greater than he
knows. It is clearly not greater than Defoe knows, however, and this
difference in knowledge constitutes one of the chief evidences of his
imaginative separateness from his character.

It is in some episodes the separateness of an ironist. And while as an
ironist in pamphlet and journal Defoe has not wanted appreciators,
critics have been slow to find irony in the novels and unwilling, when
they have found it, to credit Defoe with ironic intention. Watt, for
example, considers that what we may enjoy as irony in the novels is
merely an accidental benefit of the fact that "the course of history has

brought about in us . . . predispositions to regard certain matters ironically which Defoe and his age treated quite seriously" (p. 127). Similarly, Dobrée, who finds *Moll Flanders* "full of delicious irony so long as we keep outside Moll," questions whether Defoe himself was able to do so.[4] Coleridge, however, was confident that Defoe's ironies were intended, and he singled out for particular appreciation the scene aboard the wrecked ship in which Crusoe discovers, scornfully rejects, and, in conclusion, takes a quantity of money—compressing reflection and lapse into a few swift lines.

> I smiled to myself at the sight of this money: "O drug!" said I aloud, "What art thou good for? Thou art not worth to me, no, not the taking off of the ground; one of those knives is worth all this heap. I have no manner of use for thee; e'en remain where thou art, and go to the bottom as a creature whose life is not worth saving." However, upon second thoughts, I took it away; and wrapping all this in a piece of canvas, I began to think of making another raft. . . .

Coleridge's comment upon "I took it away" is "Worthy of Shakespeare!—and yet the simple semi-colon after it, the instant passing on without the least pause of reflex consciousness, is more exquisite and masterlike than the touch itself. A meaner writer, a Marmontel, would have put an (!) after 'away' and have commenced a fresh paragraph" (p. 155).

To this Watt has objected that editions before that of 1812, which Coleridge used, had a comma instead of a semi-colon at the crucial point, and that so unemphatic a mark of punctuation, together with the fact that the sentence rambles on to treat a number of other matters, suggests that Defoe is "hiding the effect a little too much" (p. 120), that we have, by accident of syntax, a mere "semblance of irony," not irony itself. An examination of the whole episode, however, will show a consistent ironic reserve in the attitude of the author toward his character, culminating in the comic grandiloquence of the apostrophe and its low-spoken conclusion.

In taking the money, as in all his practical activity, Crusoe behaves like an enterprising capitalist—perhaps even The Capitalist, as he seemed to Karl Marx. Such activity is, of course, necessary to sustain his life upon the island, but that it is not to be understood as an unqualified good appears both from the contradictions offered it by Crusoe's religious reflections and from Defoe's evident intention to caricature its excess. (As when Crusoe sets out to build an enclosure

---

[4] Bonamy Dobrée, "Some Aspects of Defoe's Prose," in *Pope and His Contemporaries, Essays Presented to George Sherburn,* ed. James L. Clifford and Louis A. Landa (Oxford, 1947), p. 176.

for his goats which would be two miles around: he comes late to the realization that his few goats "would be as wild in so much compass as if they had the whole island, and I shall have so much room to chase them in, that I should never catch them." Another example is the boat-building enterprise that fails because Crusoe makes his boat "big enough to have carried six and twenty men," and therefore too big to be carried to the water by one.) In the "voyages" to the wrecked ship, especially, it seems clear that Defoe has excess in view. After his second voyage Crusoe observes, "I had the biggest magazine of all kinds now that ever was laid up, I believe, for one man; but I was not satisfied still . . ." (p. 61). So he makes other voyages—twelve in all—in which he "*rummages* the cabin" and "*plunders* the ship of what was portable," bringing away "all that one pair of hands could well be supposed capable to bring, though I believe verily had the calm weather held, I should have brought away the whole ship piece by piece" (p. 62). He plunders everything, or everything "portable and fit to hand out." Beginning with the cables, "and cutting the great cable into pieces, such as I could move, I got two cables and a hawser on shore, with all the iron work I could get; and having cut down the spritsailyard, and the mizzen yard, and everything I could to make a large raft, I loaded it with all those heavy goods and came away." He does not come away without mishap, however, for the voyage ends in the near-comic catastrophe of the overreacher. "This raft was so unwieldy and so overladen, that after I was entered the little cove where I had landed the rest of my goods, not being able to guide it so handily as I did the other, it overset, and threw me and all my cargo into the water."

Finally, on his last visit to the ship, he discovers the money and denounces it in the speech applauded by Coleridge. The speech is a remarkable one, and, far from "hiding" Defoe's ironic intention, makes it brilliantly clear. To begin with, it is incredible: we cannot hear the sentiments of renunciation without scepticism from a character who has just been thrown into the water with his preposterous cargo of pillaged goods. And the language provides indications that "second thoughts" will follow. Its over-inflation ("O drug, what art thou good for?") does not suggest confidence in the attitude it urges, and it serves to invest the subject addressed—money—with a formidable authority, which is further enhanced by insistent personification. As a "creature" having "life" and addressed with four vocative pronouns in three sentences, it is clear that in Crusoe's imagination the money is a power to reckon with. And the second sentence, protesting bravely with its triple negative ("Thou art not worth to me, no, not the taking off of the ground") surely leaves the outcome of Crusoe's struggle with the money and the part of his mind that wants it in some doubt. But perhaps the most urgent reason for believing that Crusoe's revulsion is merely conventional, an attitude not so much held as wished for, is that it appears quickly to turn to love; for although he has difficulty swimming back to shore, owing to the roughness of the water and "the weight of things" about him, he has no further thought of letting the gold "go to the bottom as a creature whose life is not worth saving." And it evidently contributes to his satisfaction later, when the storm reaches its height: "I was gotten home to my little tent, where I lay with all my wealth about me very secure."

The passage is crucial not only because it shows that Defoe pre- served a distance between himself and his hero, but also because it concentrates in a little space the central irony of the book and the de- fining irony of Crusoe's inconsistent character. Dorothy Van Ghent has pointed out in her fine analysis of irony in *Moll Flanders* that Moll and her world are defined and the novel itself structured by a system of "counterstresses" corresponding to the contrary impulses of sensuality and money-getting in the main character and narrator (*The Novel, Form and Function,* New York, 1953, p. 36). There is no sensuality in Crusoe, to be sure: he has not, he tells us, "the lust of the flesh." But he shares Moll's passion for accumulation, and it is a passion similarly provided with a counterstress, his earnest spiritual purpose. The ten- sion is greater in Crusoe, however, since his contradictory impulses are more strongly opposed than Moll's. She is entirely a creature of the earth. Crusoe, on the other hand, is divided between earth and heaven, between accumulation and renunciation, action and con- templation. He is thus not merely the symbol of *homo economicus* as Watt has suggested (pp. 63–74), but of *homo* in general—perilously placed on an isthmus of a middle state and practising the indeterminate motions of a being created, in Pope's phrase, "half to rise and half to fall."

Crusoe's religion, it would seem we might insist, is the deliberate achievement of a novelist who knew what he was about. It gives the novel a higher tension and a larger resonance than Defoe's other works in fiction; and, in fact, gives a quality to the hero's experience as a "universal representative" which would seem to justify an attempt to read *Robinson Crusoe* as "myth" in a profounder sense than has yet been argued for. But the hazard of such an attempt with an author who continues to be discussed as an "unconscious artist" is obvious. As matters stand, we must sacrifice myth to consciousness; for *Robin- son Crusoe* is above all a work of conscious invention, and Defoe's in- ventive faculty was perhaps nowhere busier than with its mythic elements.

PART TWO

View Points

Karl Marx: Das Kapital

Since Robinson Crusoe's experiences are a favorite theme with political economists,[1] let us take a look at him on his island. Moderate though he be, yet some few wants he has to satisfy, and must therefore do a little useful work of various sorts, such as making tools and furniture, taming goats, fishing and hunting. Of his prayers and the like we take no account, since they are a source of pleasure to him, and he looks upon them as so much recreation. In spite of the variety of his work, he knows that his labour, whatever its form, is but the activity of one and the same Robinson, and consequently, that it consists of nothing but different modes of human labour. Necessity itself compels him to apportion his time accurately between his different kinds of work. Whether one kind occupies a greater space in his general activity than another, depends on the difficulties, greater or less as the case may be, to be overcome in attaining the useful effect aimed at. This our friend Robinson soon learns by experience, and having rescued a watch, ledger, and pen and ink from the wreck, commences, like a true-born Briton, to keep a set of books. His stock-book contains a list of the objects of utility that belong to him, of the operations necessary for their production; and lastly, of the labour time that definite quantities of those objects have, on an average, cost him. All the relations between Robinson and the objects that form this wealth of his own creation, are here so simple and clear as to be intelligible without exertion, even to Mr. Sedley Taylor. And yet those relations contain all that is essential to the determination of value.

From Karl Marx, Das Kapital (*1867*), *trans. Samuel Moore and Edward Aveling, 3 vols. (Chicago: Charles H. Kerr, 1909–10), I, 88–91.*

[1] Even Ricardo has his stories à la Robinson. "He makes the primitive hunter and the primitive fisher straightway, as owners of commodities, exchange fish and game in the proportion in which labour-time is incorporated in these exchange values. On this occasion he commits the anachronism of making these men apply to the calculation, so far as their implements have to be taken into account, the annuity tables in current use on the London Exchange in the year 1847. 'The parallelograms of Mr. Owen' appear to be the only form of society, besides the bourgeois form, with which he was acquainted." (Karl Marx, "Critique," &c., pp. 69–70.)

Let us now transport ourselves from Robinson's island bathed in light to the European middle ages shrouded in darkness. Here, instead of the independent man, we find everyone dependent, serfs and lords, vassals and suzerains, laymen and clergy. Personal dependence here characterises the social relations of production just as much as it does the other spheres of life organized on the basis of that production. But for the very reason that personal dependence forms the groundwork of society, there is no necessity for labour and its products to assume a fantastic form different from their reality. They take the shape, in the transactions of society, of services in kind and payments in kind. Here the particular and natural form of labour, and not, as in a society based on production of commodities, its general abstract form is the immediate social form of labour. Compulsory labour is just as properly measured by time, as commodity-producing labour; but every serf knows that what he expends in the service of his lord, is a definite quantity of his own personal labour-power. The tithe to be rendered to the priest is more matter of fact than his blessing. No matter, then, what we may think of the parts played by the different classes of people themselves in this society, the social relations between individuals in the performance of their labour, appear at all events as their own mutual personal relations, and are not disguised under the shape of social relations between the products of labour.

For an example of labour in common or directly associated labour, we have no occasion to go back to that spontaneously developed form which we find on the threshold of the history of all civilized races.[2] We have one close at hand in the patriarchal industries of a peasant family, that produces corn, cattle, yarn, linen, and clothing for home use. These different articles are, as regards the family, so many products of its labour, but as between themselves, they are not commodities. The different kinds of labour, such as tillage, cattle tending, spinning, weaving and making clothes, which result in the various products, are in themselves, and such as they are, direct social functions, because functions of the family, which just as much as a society based on the production of commodities, possesses a spontaneously developed system

[2] "A ridiculous presumption has latterly got abroad that common property in its primitive form is specifically a Slavonian, or even exclusively Russian form. It is the primitive form that we can prove to have existed amongst Romans, Teutons, and Celts, and even to this day we find numerous examples, ruins though they be, in India. A more exhaustive study of Asiatic, and especially of Indian forms of common property, would show how from the different forms of primitive common property, different forms of its dissolution have been developed. Thus, for instance, the various original types of Roman and Teutonic private property are deducible from different forms of Indian common property," (Karl Marx, "Critique," &c., p. 29, footnote.)

of division of labour. The distribution of the work within the family, and the regulation of the labour-time of the several members, depend as well upon differences of age and sex as upon natural conditions varying with the seasons. The labour-power of each individual, by its very nature, operates in this case merely as a definite portion of the whole labour-power of the family, and therefore, the measure of the expenditure of individual labour-power by its duration, appears here by its very nature as a social character of their labour.

Let us now picture to ourselves, by way of change, a community of free individuals, carrying on their work with the means of production in common, in which the labour-power of all the different individuals is consciously applied as the combined labour-power of the community. All the characteristics of Robinson's labour are here repeated, but with this difference, that they are social, instead of individual. Everything produced by him was exclusively the result of his own personal labour, and therefore simply an object of use for himself. The total product of our community is a social product. One portion serves as fresh means of production and remains social. But another portion is consumed by the members as means of subsistence. A distribution of this portion amongst them is consequently necessary. The mode of this distribution will vary with the productive organization of the community, and the degree of historical development attained by the producers. We will assume, but merely for the sake of a parallel with the production of commodities, that the share of each individual producer in the means of subsistence is determined by his labour-time. Labour-time would, in that case, play a double part. Its apportionment in accordance with a definite social plan maintains the proper proportion between the different kinds of work to be done and the various wants of the community. On the other hand, it also serves as a measure of the portion of the common labour borne by each individual and of his share in the part of the total product destined for individual consumption. The social relations of the individual producers, with regard both to their labour and to its products, are in this case perfectly simple and intelligible, and that with regard not only to production but also to distribution.

Roger Lloyd: The Riddle of Defoe

What is so impressive is to find in *Robinson Crusoe* the best account in the language of the tortured state of mind to which the evangelical assurance is the only answer; and of how it is that the doctrine of justification by faith does truly answer it. What is so puzzling is that this should come from the kind of man that Defoe was. One could think of no one less inherently likely to become the author of a classic of evangelical doctrine. . . . But he makes it far clearer than most works of moral theology that the real dilemma of the soul is, not any doubt of forgiveness following repentance, but that the soul wants to repent, and yet cannot manage anything more than remorse or self-contempt, or a sense of guilt. For the conductor of retreats, who must necessarily have a great deal to say about repentance, this is the really classic passage of illustration.

This evangelical theology, and this unerring piece of insight into the real need of the human soul, comes, not from Bunyan, where we might expect to find it, but from Daniel Defoe. He sounds like the last person in the world to know anything about these things. But as he did know them, why on earth is this wonderful statement of them to be found, not in one of his innumerable pamphlets, but embedded in the middle of a novel of pure romantic adventure like *Robinson Crusoe*? To place his moving discourse on spiritual despair and deliverance in such a setting was to make it as sure as possible that ninety-nine readers out of every hundred would pass by, without noticing that it was there.

How did Defoe come to know about these depths of man's spiritual nature? . . . His previous life had certainly been exceptionally varied, but in the whole range of its variety, there is nothing whatever to prepare us to find a man who seems to know almost as much as St. Augustine himself about the hidden torments of the sinful soul, and fully as much about its sense of despairing helplessness. Moreover, he could unerringly diagnose the disease as the urge to repent without the power actually to do it. He knew what some moral theologians seem to forget, that repentance is a problem first, and only afterwards a release; that it is more a free gift of God than a willed and deliberate expiation. He knew it all—and yet in all his life there is not a single hint of any repentance of his own, nor of any recognition that it might be as necessary for him as for his own Crusoe.

He was, perhaps, the greatest journalist who has ever lived, and this may have some hint of an answer to the puzzle. For no writer can be a great journalist without a sensitive and sustained imagination, and, in a writer, imagination is the power by which he is able to perceive, and even to feel, experiences in the lives of other men, which the circumstances of his own life and character have denied to him.

From Roger Lloyd, "The Riddle of Defoe," The Church Times, CXXXVII (July 16, 1954), 549. Reprinted by permission of The Church Times and the Estate of Roger Lloyd.

Truth can be approached imaginatively as well as experimentally; it can be experienced through other lives than one's own.

This, or something like it, must be what happened to Defoe, and the wonderful religious passages of *Robinson Crusoe* are the fruit of it.

Eric Berne: The Psychological Structure of Space with Some Remarks on *Robinson Crusoe*

Interest in space is a sublimation useful in many occupations. This interest has three varieties, depending upon the predominant instinctual drive it expresses: the exploration of space, the measurement of space, and the utilization of space. The interest may be intellectual, as in the case of philosophers, geometricians, and planners; or physical, as in the case of explorers, surveyors, and builders. The manifest attitude of the explorer is incorporative (this island will be incorporated into the Empire), or mastering (the conquest of Mount Everest); the surveyor insists on orderliness and exactitude; and the builder and his colleagues are intrusive (dig here, drill there), or "erective." These three interests may be characterized as predominantly oral, anal, and phallic sublimations, respectively. Although exploration is predominantly an oral sublimation, anal and phallic drives also come into play in proper sequence. The original object of exploration is not hard to discover: every child is an explorer. . . .

One of the most detailed accounts in any literature of the psychological process of organizing space into a structure is Daniel Defoe's description of Robinson Crusoe's adventures with insular fear and anxiety. Any psychoanalyst who has not reread this remarkable work since childhood may find its depth and interest far beyond his expectations. . . . Crusoe was thrown onto a strange island where he was beset with two powerful fears: "of perishing with hunger, or being devoured by wild beasts." He thinks only of getting up "into a thick bushy tree" once he has found water to drink. After he has salvaged what he can from the ship, ". . . my next work was to view the country, and seek a proper place for my habitation," where he can enclose himself in a place completely secure "from ravenous creatures, whether man or beasts." Later he begins to explore his island, both for

From *Eric Berne, M.D., "The Psychological Structure of Space with Some Remarks on* Robinson Crusoe," Psychoanalytic Quarterly, *XXV (1956), 549–57. Copyright 1956 by* Psychoanalytic Quarterly, Inc. *Reprinted by permission of the author and* Psychoanalytic Quarterly.

diversion and to seek what he can kill for food. But in the midst of all this, he feels an urgent necessity to keep his identity by maintaining his orientation in time and reckoning the days as they go by, as well as ordering his times of work, hunting, sleep, and diversion. He is also careful to determine his position in space, as precisely as he is able, by determining his latitude and longitude.

Only after he has spent ten months securing his habitation is he free "to take a more particular survey of the island itself"; and it is five years before he begins to think "of nothing but sailing round the island." This project almost ends in disaster. He is in danger of perishing "not by the sea, but of starving for hunger." By this time, the internal structure of his island is well begun. The most important loci are his plantations. The first of these is a fortification full of food with two pieces of land planted in corn; the second a similarly fortified "bower" where he keeps cattle to supply him with flesh, milk, butter, and cheese; and near by is his vineyard. He is also familiar with some points of land and some creeks into which he can run his boat safely. At this point comes one of the most dramatic moments in all literature: his discovery of a solitary human footprint on the shore. This means to him only two things: it is either the mark of the devil, or of savages who will return to devour him, or at least destroy his food supply and leave him to perish from want. Shortly afterward, his worst fears seem confirmed by the discovery of dismembered bodies and a roasting pit. For two years after that, he keeps close to his "three plantations."

All this makes him "very melancholy" and the result is that he "afterward made it a certain rule" never to fail to obey "secret hints or pressings of mind," that is, his intuition. One night, shortly after he plundered a ship wrecked near by, obtaining some very good cordials and sweetmeats and two pairs of shoes which he took off the feet of some drowned men, he reflects how for many years he has without knowing it been in real danger of "the worst kind of destruction . . . had walked about with all possible tranquility" when mere chance had preserved him from "falling into the hands of cannibals who would have seized on me with the same view as I would on a goat or turtle, and have thought it no more a crime to devour me than I did a pigeon or a curlew." He wants so badly to get away that the thought sends his very blood into a ferment; but instead of dreaming of it or "of anything relating to it," he dreams that a victim of the cannibals escapes and Crusoe carries him to his cave, thinking that this man will serve as a pilot and tell him "whither to go for provisions, and whither not to go for fear of being devoured."

When his dream comes true, one of the first things Crusoe does is make his man Friday burn the remains of the cannibal feast. He finds that Friday "had still a hankering stomach after some of the flesh." Crusoe lets him know that he will kill him if he tries it.

It is noteworthy that not only is Crusoe afraid of starving and of being eaten; he is also afraid of being poisoned by "venomous or poisonous creatures, which I might feed on to my hurt." He is grateful for being mercifully spared from these three dangers. The blessings he counts before he learns about the cannibals are as follows. "I was here removed from all the wickedness of the world; I had neither the lust of the flesh, the lust of the eye, nor the pride of life. I had nothing to covet, for I had all that I was now capable of enjoying: I was lord of the whole manor, I might call myself king or emperor over the whole country which I had possession of; there were no rivals; I had no competitor, none to dispute sovereignty or command with me." These considerations make him feel that he has made his conquest.

It is not difficult to perceive in *Robinson Crusoe* the simple fantasy of the *narrator*. The main problem is to have now all you want to eat and the indefinite assurance of future nourishment to avert the danger of starving to death. But there are the two other dangers of being poisoned and of being eaten. When you think you are secure, having possession of everything on the body of land and no one to dispute your sovereignty, along comes somebody who wants to eat you, somebody who has been lurking in the background all along and who now must be dealt with face to face. It seems that after Crusoe had incorporated his island as far as he dared through exploration and exploitation, he felt guilty; he thought the devil should surely come after him and sure enough he did. Crusoe's anxieties were based on the principle: "He who eats shall be eaten." The whole sequence of events, including his dreams, is an elaboration of this theme with familiar clinical variations. In this case, the anal and phallic elements are minimal, highly obscure, and indecisively expressed. . . .

Two types of psychological structure of geographical space are constructed by the adult. In the first the terrain is arranged beforehand by obligations which occupy the ego and form the framework for its activity, so that "exploration" becomes a subsidiary activity obscured by the more pressing obligations. In the second, exploration is an end in itself and external determinants of behavior (structure predetermined by obligations) are minimal. In the latter case, the ego is free to follow, as it were, the program of the id, and this program is a derivative of archaic patterns.

In so far, then, as exploration is a productive or a creative activity, it becomes an art. Like all the arts it is restricted by its medium, but within those restrictions its creativity is the result of guidance from the id and represents a sublimation of pregenital strivings. In [the case of *Robinson Crusoe*], neurotic fixations restrict the productivity. Crusoe, because of his oral fixation and the accompanying intense anxiety, never did explore the whole extent of his island effectively.

Maximillian E. Novak: The Economic Meaning of *Robinson Crusoe*

Many writers on economics and politics had located their utopias on islands isolated from Western civilization, but it was Defoe's unique contribution to begin with the single man. Six years before *Robinson Crusoe*, in his *General History of Trade*, Defoe argued that although God had created the world in such a way as to make commerce essential, he might have done it so that "every Man should have been his own Labourer, or his own Manufacturer." [1] But whereas God assured each country its share of the necessities of life, he spread the articles needed for comfort and convenience all over the earth. It is interesting that the idea of economic isolation occurred to Defoe several months after a sailor named Alexander Selkirk returned to England and achieved some notoriety for having spent more than four years in isolation on the island of Juan Fernández.

In the *General History of Trade* there is also a variation on an old proverb that appears innumerable times throughout Defoe's writings. "Necessity," he wrote, "which is the Mother, and Convenience which is the Handmaid of Invention, first Directed Mankind . . . to Contrive, Supplies and Support of Life." [2] This proverb is the key to an economic doctrine that probably had its origins in Machiavelli's dictum, "Men never do good unless necessity drives them to it." [3] Sir William Temple expanded on this idea in his *Observations upon the United Provinces,* suggesting that inventions probably increased after men had moved to the city, where those who had no way of supporting life resorted to their personal ingenuity to find some means to survive. Defoe knew Temple's work well, but he probably took his theory from John Asgil, who went beyond Temple in asserting that "All the Improvements in the World have been produced from the Necessity of

---

From Maximillian E. Novak, Economics and the Fiction of Daniel Defoe *(Berkeley and Los Angeles: University of California Press, 1962), pp. 49–50, 53–60, 62–66. Reprinted by permission of the publisher.*

[1] *A General History of Trade* (London, 1713), no. 1, p. 33.

[2] *Ibid.,* p. 31.

[3] Niccolò Machiavelli, *The Discourses,* trans. Leslie J. Walker (London, 1950), I 217.

Men, putting them upon Invention." [4] Under Asgil's influence Defoe, in his *Essay upon Projects*, expanded this idea by arguing that when faced by "Necessity" men must find some means of surviving, and that these are usually fraud, theft, or honest invention. It was necessity alone, Defoe argued, which destroyed sloth and gave birth to society. . . .

One critic has contended that Defoe believed in the Calvinist conception of work as a proof of salvation, but there is little evidence to support this.[5] It would be more accurate to state that Defoe seems to have believed that most men had a drive to work, or an "instinct of workmanship" accompanied by a hatred of idleness.[6] "A Life of Sloth and Idleness," wrote Defoe, "is not Happiness or Comfort; Employment is Life, Sloth and Indolence is Death; to be busy, is to be chearful, to be pleasant; to have nothing to do, is all Dejection, dispiriting, and a word, to be fit for nothing but Mischief and the Devil." [7] This suggestion also seems to confuse labor and work. Crusoe's father is a great exponent of steady work in one's calling, but he has a certain contempt and horror for the life of the laborer, with its physical pains and sufferings. Crusoe, however, prefers this type of work to idleness, and it seems to be part of his character rather than part of his religion. Even if he feels that his labor on the island is a calling that God has chosen for him, this hardly explains his activity. Indeed, the only direct connection between religion and work in *Robinson Crusoe* relates to his loss of time in the supererogation of reading the Bible and his insistence on resting one day in seven. Certainly Crusoe's fear of the supernatural—his belief that the devil has visited his island—almost destroys his efficiency as a workman.[8] . . .

That labor and invention create things of use and that the value of things depends on their utility are the economic themes of Crusoe's life on his island. These ideas were far from being new, and their main exponent was the most famous philosopher of the time, John Locke. In his *Two Treatises on Civil Government* Locke advanced the idea that value was not inherent in nature, but was created out of it by human labor. "For whatever bread is more worth than acorns," he wrote, "wine than water, and cloths or silk than leaves, skins or moss,

---

[4] *Several Assertions Proved* (London, 1696), pp. 4–8.

[5] Ian Watt, *The Rise of the Novel* (London, 1957), p. 74.

[6] This is Veblen's term. See *Theory of the Leisure Class* (New York, 1934), p. 93.

[7] *A Plan of the English Commerce* (Shakespeare Head ed.), p. 52.

[8] Believing that the footprint in the sand is the work of the Devil, Crusoe stops working at his inventions and hides in fear. Even after he discovers a natural cause in the visits of cannibals to his island, he is never able to regain his pleasure in invention and handicrafts. See *Robinson Crusoe*, I, 194.

that is wholly owing to labour and industry." [9] As an example Locke pointed to the American Indians, whose land was untilled and supported few inhabitants, and was consequently almost worthless. . . .

When placed in a condition of necessity, therefore, Crusoe uses his ingenuity to duplicate all the tasks required to sustain civilized society. Through his prudence, inherited from, or transmitted by, his early life as the son of a wealthy tradesman, he succeeds in creating capital. Rousseau, who decided that it was agriculture and not money which removed man from the state of nature, argued that no natural savage would throw away seeds in the present with an expectation of future profit.[10] But Crusoe is willing to create his wealth by means of roundabout processes. He is not content with the acorns, the berries, and the water of the savage. In spite of his environment, Crusoe's life is that of Rousseau's civilized man: "Always moving, sweating, toiling, and racking his brains to find still more laborious occupations: he goes on in drudgery to his last moment, and even seeks death to put himself in a position to live." [11] Defoe almost reverses the process of the *voyage imaginaire;* instead of sending his civilized man back to nature for reformation, as Neville did in his *Isle of Pines,* Defoe creates an interaction between man and nature by which nature was to be made more productive and man more pure. . . .

Actually, although Defoe recognized the effect of labor on Crusoe's environment, he seems to have been more concerned with a utility theory of value than a labor theory. Here again Defoe followed Locke's concept of economic life in the state of nature, where to keep things that one could not use was a sin and where gold was useless. "In the beginning," Locke wrote, "before the desire of having more than men needed had altered the intrinsic value of things, which depends only on their usefulness to the life of man, . . . though men had a right to appropriate by their labour, . . . as much of the things of Nature as he could use, yet this could not be much, nor to the prejudice of others. . . ." [12] Thus Crusoe muses on his vast resources of timber and the potentialities for growing food on his island. He might be able to feed an army or build a fleet, but to exploit his land beyond what he personally needs would be futile:

> But all I could make use of, was All that was valuable. I had enough to eat, and to supply my Wants, and, what was all the rest to me?

[9] (Everyman Library ed.; London, 1955), p. 137.
[10] *A Discourse,* in *The Social Contract,* trans. G. D. H. Cole (Everyman Library ed.; London, n.d.), p. 200.
[11] *Ibid.,* p. 220.
[12] *Two Treatises,* p. 134.

If I kill'd more Flesh than I could eat, the Dog must eat it, or the
Vermin. If I sow'd more Corn than I could eat, it must be spoil'd.
The Trees that I cut down, were lying to rot on the Ground. I could
make no more use of them than for Fewel; and that I had no Occasion
for, but to dress my Food. (I, 149)

The paradox of the uselessness of gold and the utility theory of
value had even greater attractions for Defoe's mind. The concept, of
course, was almost a commonplace and probably the main theory of
value before Adam Smith. In 1690 Nicholas Barbon had argued that
the "Value of all Wares arise from their Use; Things of no Use, have
no Value, as the *English* Phrase is, *They are good for nothing.*" [13] Defoe
could never bring himself to regard gold as valueless, but he did contend that it was merely a medium of trade established by custom. In
discussing the trade to Africa, he remarked that the natives "willingly
Barter, their Gold, *as a useless Trifle to them,* for the much more
valuable Toy of a Cowry or Little Shell, fit here only for the use of
our Children, and hardly valuable by them. . . ." [14] Even in his
highest praise of gold, Defoe seldom confused the use value of goods
with their money price, but he agreed with Locke that because gold and
silver had intrinsic value, they were the best mediums of exchange.

It is with these ideas in mind that one must read Crusoe's most
famous speech (Coleridge compared it to Shakespeare):

I smil'd to my self at the Sight of this Money, O Drug! Said I aloud,
what art thou good for, Thou art not worth to me, no not the taking
off of the Ground, one of those Knives is worth all this Heap, I have
no Manner of use for thee; e'en remain where thou art, and go to the
Bottom as a Creature whose Life is not worth saving. However, upon
Second Thoughts, I took it away. . . . (I, 64)

Professor Watt has attacked Coleridge's judgment on the grounds that
it was not an appropriate speech for Crusoe to make and that the
irony was accidental.[15] But this speech is only inappropriate if one
accepts the idea that Crusoe is really exploiting the island as a capitalist. Actually Crusoe's rejection of the money is merely a paradoxical
statement of the uselessness of money in the state of nature. And
Crusoe can afford to sneer at a commodity that he never pursued with
any steadiness. A better interpretation of Crusoe's character makes his
speech entirely understandable, for if the romantic in Crusoe can con-

---

[13] *A Discourse of Trade,* ed. Jacob H. Hollander (Baltimore, 1934), p. 13.

[14] *Review,* III, 9b.

[15] See Samuel Taylor Coleridge, *Miscellaneous Criticism,* ed. Thomas Raysor
(Cambridge, Mass., 1934), p. 293; and Watt, *op. cit.,* pp. 119–20.

demn the money, the prudent streak in his nature cannot resist the temptation to take it away. There can be no question that Defoe was being ironic about his hero's pretensions, although Defoe probably shared Crusoe's wavering feelings toward the gold. . . .

Defoe concurs with the natural-law philosophers, Grotius and Pufendorf, that islands in the sea belong to whoever first seizes or discovers them.[16] Like Rousseau, Defoe may have associated this process with agriculture. Crusoe's realization of his proprietorship and kingship follows shortly after his discovery of the sprouts of grain, thrown casually in a spot where they happen to grow. Since Crusoe distinctly believes that both the grain and the tools which enable him to survive are signs of God's favor to him, he may feel that he has a "divine right" to his island.[17] . . .

Rousseau contended that Crusoe was indeed absolute king of his island, but only so long as he was the only human inhabitant. And almost all the English political philosophers who followed Locke would have agreed that no king has absolute power over the property of his subjects. It is clear, however, that Defoe was not a disciple of Locke in this matter. In a British Museum copy of Defoe's *Original Power of the Collective Body of the People of England,* a contemporary reader, imbued with Whig principles, has made approving marginal comments on all Defoe's remarks except for a curious contention that a foreign nation might buy all the land in England and thereby purchase it out of existence.[18] The anonymous reader realized that this was a principle of property which far exceeded the fetishism of Locke. . . .

When Crusoe decides to settle the colony along permanent lines, he does not give the land away to the colonists, but following closely Defoe's plan for a colony of Palatine immigrants in the forested areas of England, he rents his property with long leases and deferred payment.[19] Defoe believed that any group of workers gathered in one spot would create wealth through the cycle of production and consumption. There is nothing communistic about Crusoe's colony; the

---

[16] See Hugo Grotius, *De Jure Belli ac Pacis,* trans. Francis W. Kelsey (Oxford, 1925), II, 301.

[17] Defoe would probably have called it a "natural right." His attitude toward man's right to property was traditional. Cf. Defoe, *Lex Talionis,* in *A Collection of the Writings of the Author of the True-Born English-Man* (London, 1703), p. 248, and Thorstein Veblen, *Absentee Ownership* (New York, 1923), pp. 21–60. See also *A Fourth Essay, at Removing National Prejudices* (Edinburgh, 1706), p. 11.

[18] (London, 1702 [1701]), p. 19 (British Museum, 193.d.14.[26]).

[19] *A Tour through England and Wales* (Everyman Library ed.; London, 1928), I, 200–206.

concepts of degree and economic class run through it in strong lines. Already diligence has separated the rich from the poor and, to some extent, color has divided the ruling class from their inferiors. Crusoe's utopia emerges as almost the exact opposite of Gonzalo's reconstruction of the "Golden Age" in *The Tempest*.

Crusoe is an extraordinarily capable, if entirely human, man whose greatest difficulty is his inability to remain at one occupation. He is a shrewd merchant, a skilled craftsman, and a tough-minded colonizer, but as a "True Born Englishman" of the age of voyaging and exploration, Crusoe prefers to wander.

It is also apparent that Defoe transmuted his economic theories into fiction in much the same manner as he fictionalized his economic tracts. To conjecture whether he conceived his story first, as a fictional voyage, and only afterward embellished it with various economic themes, or whether he conceived the idea of economic isolation first, would be as futile as to debate over the primacy of the chicken and the egg. But there is no question that, more often than not, Defoe created his fiction from ideas rather than from incidents. Saintsbury's dictum that a man would rather hang than read Defoe for anything but his stories was hardly among his most perspicacious judgments, for the excellence of Defoe's stories depends not upon the stringing together of disjointed incidents but upon a profound knowledge of the implications of his material. . . .

George A. Starr: Robinson Crusoe and the Myth of Mammon

What we make of the hero's labors greatly influences our response to *Robinson Crusoe*. Indeed, from Rousseau's day to our own, most differences of interpretation are traceable to this single factor, the varying significance attached to Crusoe's work.[1] One recent commentator, for instance, finds implicit in it the creed of the dignity of labor: on his reading, Crusoe's efforts signify that the human lot is heroic only when productive, and that man is capable of redemption

From George A. Starr, Defoe and Spiritual Autobiography (Princeton, New Jersey: Princeton University Press, 1965), pp. 185–86, 192–97. Reprinted by permission of the publisher.

[1] See Charles Eaton Burch, "British Criticism of Defoe as a Novelist, 1719–1860," *E.S.*, Vol. 67 (1932), pp. 178–98, and "Defoe's British Reputation 1869–1894," *E.S.*, Vol. 68 (1934), pp. 410–23.

only through untiring labor. "If we draw a moral," this critic maintains, "it can only be that for all the ailments of man and his society, Defoe confidently prescribes the therapy of work." [2]

We may question, however, whether such an interpretation does justice either to Defoe's intention or to the facts of the narrative. The ideology here ascribed to Defoe had found expression long before the appearance of *Robinson Crusoe*: Mammon, after all, is traditionally its most eloquent advocate. It is he who counsels his fellows in Pandaemonium not to attempt further insurrections,

> but rather seek
> Our own good from ourselves, and from our own
> Live to ourselves, though in this vast recess,
> Free, and to none accountable, preferring
> Hard liberty before the easie yoke
> Of servil Pomp. Our greatness will appear
> Then most conspicuous, when great things of small,
> Useful of hurtful, prosperous of adverse,
> We can create, and in what place so e're
> Thrive under evil, and work ease out of pain
> Through labour and endurance.[3]

To be sure, Milton makes clear from the outset that Mammon is "the least erected Spirit that fell from Heav'n"; yet some modern criticism would have us see such a figure in Robinson Crusoe.

In my opinion there is a vast difference in spirit between Mammon, that prototypical *homo economicus,* and the regenerate Crusoe. . . . What is to be avoided is the extreme position of those who, in Samuel Clarke's words, "rely with such confidence on the Effects of their own Wisdom and Industry, and so presumptuously depend upon the natural and regular Tendencies of second Causes; as if they thought, either there was no Superior Cause at all, on which the Frame of Nature depended; or at least, that the Providence of God did not condescend to direct the Events of Things, in this lower and uncertain World." [4] Industry, then, has no intrinsic merit; it becomes

---

[2] Ian Watt, *"Robinson Crusoe* as a Myth," pp. 165, 166 and *passim; The Rise of the Novel,* pp. 72–74. Cf. Max Weber, *The Protestant Ethic and the Spirit of Capitalism* (N.Y., 1958), pp. 171–72 and *passim.*

[3] John Milton, *Paradise Lost,* II, 252–62, in *Poetical Works,* edited by Helen Darbishire, 2 vols. (Oxford, 1952), I, 32–33.

[4] "The Event of Things not always answerable to Second Causes," in *Sermons,* VI, 187–89. The proper relation between diligence and dependence had been summed up memorably by Donne a century earlier in the third verse letter "To

valuable only when coupled with an acknowledgment of God's ultimate power to further or thwart it. Mammon's independence and self-
reliance, far from being redeeming features, are at the very core of
his iniquity, since they involve a denial of God's sovereignty.[5] . . .

It remains to show that Crusoe, following his conversion, comes
to fulfill this ideal, rather than the one embodied and proposed by
Spenser's and Milton's Mammon. The first thing to consider is
Crusoe's behavior between his shipwreck and his conversion. . . .
Two episodes can be singled out which seem to characterize them all,
up to the time of his conversion: the springing up of the barley
affords one kind of commentary on his efforts, the partial destruction
of his cave by earthquake another.

Near his fortification Crusoe shakes out a grain-bag, in which he
sees nothing but husks and dust; after the rainy season he finds barley
growing on the spot. Dry husks drove the prodigal back to his
father's home, and ten or twelve ears of green English barley nearly
have the same effect on Crusoe. At first he takes this for a miracle, and
begins to bless himself that such a prodigy of nature should happen
on his account; he is ready to acknowledge himself the beneficiary of
Providence. But when he recalls shaking out the bag in that place,
he confesses that "the wonder began to cease" and "my religious
thankfulness began to abate too, upon the discovering that all this
was nothing but what was common." As he goes on to reflect, however,
"I ought to have been thankful for so strange and unforeseen providence, as if it had been miraculous, for it really was the work of Providence as to me" (pp. 84–86). In other words, he relapses quickly into
what he himself later condemns as an exclusive attention to second

The Countesse of Bedford" (*Poetical Works,* edited by H. J. C. Grierson [Oxford,
1912], p. 173):

> Who prayer-lesse labours, or without this, prayes,
> Doth but one halfe, that's none; He which said, *Plough*
> *And looke not back,* to looke up doth allow.

Donne alludes to Luke 9:62; John Flavel was to make a similar point in *The
Seaman's Companion* (1676), in *Whole Works,* II, 267.

[5] Compare Benjamin Whichcote, "The Conversion of a Sinner," in *Works,* I, 218:
"It was never God's intention when he made man at first, to put him into a state
of absolute *independency,* or *self-sufficiency.* And therefore whosoever assumes it to
himself, doth assume that which never did belong to a creature-state."

Mammon is guilty of that kind of "thoughtfulness for the morrow" that necessarily proceeds, as John Howe expresses it, "from an ungovernable spirit, a heart
not enough subdued to the ruling power of God in the world." Howe's treatise
"Of Thoughtfulness for the Morrow," first published in 1681, is one of the most
systematic explorations of this whole question: see his *Works,* pp. 328–48, esp. p.
333f.

causes; he fails to look beyond them to a first cause. He is still the "dunghill wretch" Thomas Lye spoke of, who attributes a crop to natural causes rather than thanking God for it." [6]

The relation between Crusoe's own efforts and God's doing also emerges clearly from the earthquake episode. With his improvised tools, Crusoe struggles to make his cave "spacious enough to accommodate [him] as a warehouse or magazine, a kitchen, a dining-room, and a cellar." In eight minutes an earthquake threatens to ruin the work of six months. But once again, he fails to see God's hand in the matter. As he later remarks, "though nothing could be more terrible in its nature, or more immediately directing to the invisible Power, which alone directs such things, yet no sooner was the first fright over, but the impression it had made went off also." [7] Thus he repeats his error over the barley. In the former case, Providence had made the most casual action fruitful; in the latter, Providence negates his most assiduous toils. Each episode minimizes, in a different way, the role of Crusoe's own efforts, and correspondingly magnifies the role of Providence. On both occasions Crusoe frustrates the divine intention, for neither blessing nor alarm brings him to a sense of his dependence on God.

Eventually he does gain this awareness; what happens, in fact, is that the labors of the regenerate Crusoe come to fulfill the wishes of the divines quoted earlier. After conversion he does not slacken his efforts, but goes about them in an altogether different spirit. Recognizing that providence plays a decisive and benign role in all his affairs, he learns thankfulness and resignation. Previously, he reports, "the anguish of my soul at my condition would break out upon me on a sudden, and my very heart would die within me. . . . In the midst of the greatest composures of my mind, this would break out upon me like a storm, and make me wring my hands, and weep like a child" (p. 125). But now, comforted by the Biblical assurance that "I will never, never leave thee, nor forsake thee," Crusoe attains a serenity that no subsequent crises and alarms can long interrupt. It is not the therapy of work that confers this security, but the realization that he

[6] On the necessity of distinguishing between "second causes" and a "first cause," see Richard Baxter, *The Divine Life* (1664), in *Practical Works* (1830), XIII, 32; Isaac Barrow, "On the Gunpowder Treason," in *Theological Works* (Oxford, 1859), I, 448–49; Samuel Clarke, *Sermons*, X, 11–12; Joseph Hall, *Works*, VIII, 28–29. Defoe himself frequently deplored, as in the *Review*, I (IX), 2, that "second Causes have the Blessings or Curses of every Action, without any regard to the great first moving Cause of all Things."

[7] Pp. 79, 83, 87, 81, 99; cf. p. 88, where Crusoe says, "All this while I had not the least serious religious thought, nothing but the common 'Lord, have mercy upon me!' and when it was over, that went away too."

is the object of what one bishop calls "that special providence of God, which is man's only security." [8] He gains a sense of well-being, not through purposive possession, but through understanding that God has furnished him a table in the wilderness.[9] What affords him peace of mind is not his success in the role of *homo economicus,* but the discovery that he can rely on Providence for direction and support. By making himself amenable to expressions of the divine will, by becoming alert and tractable, he can at once avail himself of divine assistance, and free himself of the immoderate care rebuked in the Sermon on the Mount. If, as Mr. Watt rightly observes, Crusoe "turns his forsaken estate into a triumph," it is less through sheer labor than through acquiring a sense of dependence; and it is this sense of God's concern and provision for him that keeps such a triumph from being, as Mr. Watt finds it, "a flagrant unreality." [10] For, as Coleridge observed long ago, "The carpentering, tailoring, pottery, are all just what will answer his purpose, and those are confined to needs that all men have, and comforts all men desire. Crusoe rises only where all men may be made to feel that they might and that they ought to rise —in religion, in resignation, in dependence on, and thankful acknowledgment of the divine mercy and goodness." [11]

J. Paul Hunter: [The Un-sources of *Robinson Crusoe*]

The artistry of *Robinson Crusoe* is most seriously maligned, however, not by viewing the novel's parts as somehow dependent upon travel books, but by considering its total form to be patterned on the travel tradition. Source hunters did not set out specifically to "place" *Robinson Crusoe* within any literary tradition, but, because they failed to distinguish between what Defoe worked from (sources) and what

From *J. Paul Hunter,* The Reluctant Pilgrim (*Baltimore: The Johns Hopkins Press, 1966*), *pp. 113–19. Reprinted by permission of the publisher.*

[8] George Bull, *Works,* I, 470; cf. Crane, *Isagoge,* pp. 16, 160–61, and 523.

[9] In three places Crusoe echoes the passage from Psalm 78:19: see pp. 104, 143, 164. Compare also the allusion to Elijah and the Ravens (I Kings 17:4–6) at p. 146. In his Autobiography (1711), Robert Knox meditates on the same text: see *An Historical Relation of Ceylon together With somewhat concerning Severall Remarkeable passages of my life that hath hapned since my Deliverance out of my Captivity,* edited by James Ryan (Glasgow, 1911), p. 400.

[10] *"Robinson Crusoe* as a Myth," p. 167.

[11] *Coleridge's Miscellaneous Criticism,* edited by T. M. Raysor (Cambridge, Mass., 1936), p. 300.

he worked toward (artistic aims), their conclusions have had the effect of defining *Robinson Crusoe* itself as a fictionalized travel book.[1] Such a definition has serious implications for the structure and meaning of *Robinson Crusoe*, as today's critical commonplaces about the novel clearly demonstrate, for, like the Selkirk conjecture, it suggests that Defoe's art is fact-centered rather than idea-centered. Because questionable assumptions and procedures have led to such a definition, the validity of the conclusion is at least doubtful, but ultimately such a definition has to rest (as Shakespearean studies ought to have taught us) not upon the matter of source materials at all, but upon questions of Defoe's aims and those of the travel writers. Examined on this basis, the categorizing of *Robinson Crusoe* as travel literature is even less valid than other conclusions of Defoe source studies, for (aside from a few surface similarities) *Robinson Crusoe* makes no attempt to follow the conventional pattern of the travel tradition.

Despite their subliterary status, travel books early in the seventeenth century developed a set of distinguishing characteristics almost as rigid as the conventions of a poetic genre: each book tried to answer the same kinds of questions and each was organized in much the same way. Travel books depended for their success on the continued interest of a buying public with specific expectations, and even when their stated purpose was to offer other benefits, travel writers usually fulfilled those expectations.[2] "I know 'tis generally expected," writes Woodes Rogers in his introduction to *A Cruising Voyage Round the World*, "that when far distant Voyages are printed, they should contain new and wonderful Discovries with surprizing Accounts of People and Animals,"[3] and like other voyagers, Rogers condemns this popular taste. But, also like others, he satisfies the very expectations which he rails against. . . .

Basically, the formula may be described as chronological in movement from place to place, topical in describing the particulars of each place. Much geographical detail is given about the places and about the natives and their customs, but there is relatively little emphasis on event. When an unusual happening (like the finding of Selkirk) is

[1] Even Professor Secord fails to make this important distinction, and slips into a "placing" of *Robinson Crusoe* based on sources: " 'Robinson Crusoe,' finally, is not so much a fictitious autobiography . . . as it is a fictitious book of travel . . ." (p. 111).

[2] Reader expectation was, of course, largely determined by familiarity with Hakluyt, Purchas, and their seventeenth-century successors. For a good recent account of travel literature, see Percy G. Adams, *Travelers and Travel Liars* (Berkeley and Los Angeles, 1962).

[3] P. xiv.

described, the tone retains the same calm, dispassionate quality that characterizes the rest of the book, for "objectivity" of tone and style characterizes the tradition as a whole.[4] An important aspect of this objectivity is the absence of any informing idea of theme: chronology, replaced by topicality when the narrative is interrupted to describe a particular place, is the only organizing force in the books, thematic considerations being inappropriate to the "pose" or conventions of the form.[5]

Secord notes that Defoe has Crusoe "do a series of things well known in the literature of travel; suffer storm and shipwreck, endure slavery . . . , duplicate the experiences of desert island life, and participate in both commerce and travel," but the resemblances, as Secord's comparison would suggest, are broad ones.[6] Crusoe describes events in chronological order (after a rationale for the first voyage is established) until the "narrator" returns home from his longest, most arduous voyage. The style is matter-of-fact, and the book contains some of the same kinds of "fact" as do the travel books. When Crusoe is at sea, he frequently gives his position, speed, and direction; on land, he describes the animals and the weapons, food, and customs of the natives. About his island he gives full information, detailing its geography, climatic patterns, animal and plant life, and the sailing conditions around it.

But these superficial similarities lose their significance when one notes Defoe's very different emphasis and his considerably different

[4] See, for example, the Hakluyt Society edition of Lionel Wafer's *A New Voyage & Description of the Isthmus of America* (ed. L. E. Elliott Joyce [Oxford, 1934]), in which the contrast between Wafer's "Secret Report" and the published version of his travels suggests the tone and manner expected of a narrator in travel literature.

[5] The typical narrative first states the author's credentials (previous sea experience) and explains the nature and purpose of the current voyage. The ship is described (size, number and type of sails), and often the more important members of the crew are introduced. The log of days at sea is detailed enough for a curious reader to trace the journey; masses of information are given about daily locations, winds, currents, and factors affecting the speed and direction of the voyage. Unusual events (storms, sighting of other ships, dietary problems, pirate encounters, crew changes) sometimes are given extended treatment, but such anecdotes seldom extend beyond two or three pages. On the other hand, topical descriptions of places and peoples visited are usually lengthy. The amount of detail for each place varies, of course, with the knowledge of the voyager and with the general importance of the particular place, but ordinarily such matters as the kinds of fish inhabiting the coastal waters or native methods of building huts get far more attention than any event. Such information may or may not have sold the books, but travel writers at least pretend to think it did.

[6] Secord, *Studies*, p. 109. The superficiality of the similarities suggests that instead of attempting to imitate the style and format of travel books (which the author of *The Shortest Way with the Dissenters* could surely do, if he tried) Defoe used features like the title page simply to attract a particular kind of reader, one who was perhaps unlikely to be reached by *The Family Instructor*.

use of similar materials. In *Robinson Crusoe* the facts about various places are never presented as information for its own sake; each fact is introduced because of its function in the narrative situation. Lions and leopards are described in Africa because they represent, in one case, danger to Crusoe and Xury, and, in another, their means of reciprocating the kindness of the natives. The description of the island accumulates gradually as the narrative unfolds; there is no tabular itemizing of descriptive facts. And the island is the only land area which receives anything like a full description. About Brazil the reader learns only a few things pertinent to Crusoe; during the voyage from Sallee, he is given only facts necessary to the narrative. Here, the description serves the narrative; in the travel books, the narrative often merely connects the various descriptions, which are avowedly the most important parts.

Failure to define the rationale and mode of the travel books has led to a general lack of discrimination between various kinds of books concerned with discovery.[7] *Robinson Crusoe* clearly is more like contemporary adventure stories than like the travel books; information is subordinated to event, and the movement is dramatic. Chronology, simply a convenience in the travel books, becomes for Defoe (as for adventure stories) a conscious device to dramatize development.[8] But

[7] Throughout this study, I use the term "travel literature" to refer only to published reports of such explorers as Dampiers, Rogers, and Cooke. This kind of literature was the chief type used by source students in their work; Secord, for example, lists ten such books as "certain" or "probable" sources of *Robinson Crusoe* and its two sequels. However, he also includes Defoe's *The Storm* and the anonymous *Providence Displayed* as sources of the same type.

The term travel literature is sometimes used in a broader, less precise sense; a recent English Institute program on travel literature contained, for example, a paper on science fiction (as voyages of the mind). Under a broad enough definition of the term, *The Pilgrim's Progress, The Odyssey,* and almost every eighteenth-century novel could fit the category. But it is important to distinguish between different types of publications dealing with travel, and because source students have usually used the term "travel literature" to refer to reports like Dampier's, I have retained their term here. I use it, however, *only* to describe writings like Dampier's, not those with different aims and methods.

[8] Adventure stories often involve travel to far-off places, but travel books seldom involve much adventure. When writers like Dampier or Cooke do describe exciting events, they de-emphasize the action in accordance with their avowal that their only concern is information. Events only explain delays in the voyage or difficulties of exploration: they do not structure a sequential relation. Chronology is less a conscious structure than a convenience. Adventure stories—factual or fictional, episodic or unified—use chronology to suggest movement; they depend upon a world of time, for they are concerned with event, not fact. Even when based on actual happenings, they obviously filter and formulate experience, organizing it in a more or less dramatic manner; travel books, by contrast, pretend to be almost photographic. The difference is that between a story and a report.

even more important, *Robinson Crusoe* has a larger coherence than that produced by the narrative sequence—a coherence which ultimately separates *Robinson Crusoe* from both travel literature and adventure stories, for books in both the latter traditions lack an informing idea which gives a meaning to individual events or to the sequence as a whole. These books seem to lack ideological content, and no thematic meaning can be abstracted from them. Some critics have insisted that *Robinson Crusoe* resembles them in this respect, that it is episodic and lacks fundamental unity. Secord states as a truism that *Robinson Crusoe* "imitates life in its very shapelessness." [9] This view, however, ignores the thematic structure of the novel, a structure set up by the artistic (and ultimately philosophical) rationale for all of Crusoe's wanderings.

Crusoe is never merely an adventurer who goes from place to place, participating in isolated events. Each of his experiences takes on meaning in relation to a pattern set in motion by his "fatal . . . Propension of Nature" (A2)—an irrational inclination to roam. His "rambling Thoughts" (A1) cause him to rebel against parental authority and against his divinely appointed "station"—a rebellion which he interprets as his "Original Sin" (A225). Crusoe views each subsequent tragic event as punishment for his rebellion, and at last concludes that real deliverance from his plight (both physical and spiritual) is only possible when he resigns himself completely to the will of God.

[9] P. 232.

Chronology of Important Dates

	Defoe	Historical Events
1660	Daniel Defoe [exact date un-known] born in London.	Restoration of Charles II.
1665		68,500 deaths in the Great Plague of London.
Sept. 1666		The Great Fire of London destroyed two-thirds of the city.
1670's	attended the Rev. James Fisher's school, Dorking, Surrey.	
1674?– 1679?	attended the Rev. Charles Morton's academy, Newington Green, Middlesex, to prepare for Presbyterian ministry.	
1678– 1681		The Popish Plot to restore Roman Catholicism in England.
1683?	set up in import-export business in Freeman's Yard, Cornhill, London.	
1683	published 1st political tract (no copy known).	
Jan. 1684	married Mary Tuffley, said to be daughter of a wine-cooper, with a dowry of £3700.	
Feb. 1685		Charles II succeeded by his Roman Catholic brother, James II.
June 1685	joined Protestant Duke of Monmouth's rebellion in Somersetshire.	
1685– 1692	travelled frequently throughout England and the continent on business.	

Jan. 1688	admitted to the Butcher's Company, a trade guild.	
1688	published first extant political tract against James II (Moore, 5).	
Nov.–Dec. 1688		William, Prince of Orange, landed at Torbay, Devonshire. James II fled London. Louis XIV declared war on England.
Dec. 1688	rode to Henley to join advancing forces of William.	
1692	wartime losses of shipping which Defoe had insured forced him into bankruptcy for £17,000.	
Sept. 1697		Treaty of Ryswick concluded between France and England.
Jan. 1701	published *The True-Born Englishman* in defense of William III.	
May 1701	presented *Legion's Memorial* to Robert Harley, Speaker of the House of Commons.	
Dec. 1701	youngest child, Sophia, baptized.	
March 1702		William III succeeded by Queen Anne.
May 1702		England declared war on France over the Spanish Succession.
1703	arrested for publishing a seditious libel, *The Shortest Way with the Dissenters* (1702), attacking Church of England for persecuting dissenters. Imprisoned, heavily fined, and exposed in the pillory.	
Nov. 1703	released from Newgate prison by Robert Harley, for whom Defoe undertook propaganda and intelligence work until 1714.	
Feb. 1704–	wrote the *Review*, a bi-weekly journal of opinion.	

June	
1713	
Aug.	Marlborough's victory over the French at Blenheim, in Bavaria.
1704	
1706–10	frequently in Scotland.
May	Marlborough's victory at Ramillies, in Brabant.
1706	
March	Act of Union between Scotland and England.
1707	
c. Jan.	moved to Stoke Newington, suburb north of London, where he lived the rest of his life.
1708	
July	Marlborough's victory at Oudenarde, in Flanders.
1708	
1713	repeatedly arrested by Harley's political enemies, once for publishing *And what if the Pretender should come?* and two more ironical tracts in support of the Hanoverian Succession.
Aug.	Fall of Harley ministry. Queen Anne succeeded by George I, of Hanover.
1714	
March	published *The Family Instructor,* first didactic treatise.
1715	
1715–30	undertook propaganda and intelligence work for successive Whig ministries.
April	published *The Life and Strange Surprizing Adventures of Robinson Crusoe of York, Mariner.*
25, 1719	
June	published *The Life, Adventures, and Pyracies or the Famous Captain Singleton.*
1720	
Jan.	published *The Fortune and Misfortunes of the Famous Moll Flanders.*
1722	
March	published *A Journal of the Plague Year.*
1722	
Dec.	published *The History and Remarkable Life of the Truly Honourable Col. Jacque.*
1722	

Feb. 1724	published *The Fortunate Mistress: Or . . . Roxana.*	
June 1727		George I succeeded by George II.
April 24, 1731	died in Ropemaker's Alley, hiding from creditors.	

Notes on the Editor and Contributors

EDWIN B. BENJAMIN (1916–   ), professor of English literature at Temple University, has published *The Province of Poetry* (1966) and more than a dozen articles in the learned journals. He is a former member of the Harvard Cooperative Society.

ERIC BERNE, M.D. (1910–   ) is a practicing psychiatrist whose works include *The Structure and Dynamics of Organizations and Groups* (1963) and *Games People Play* (1964).

FRANK H. ELLIS (1916–   ), editor of this volume, is professor of English literature at Smith College. He is also the editor of Swift's *Discourse of the Contests and Dissentions* (1967) and of two volumes covering the reign of Queen Anne in the Yale *Poems on Affairs of State* series.

WILLIAM H. HALEWOOD (1929–   ) teaches at the University of Toronto. His special interests are 17th and 18th century literature.

J. PAUL HUNTER (1934–   ), the author of *The Reluctant Pilgrim: Defoe's Emblematic Method and the Quest for Form in* Robinson Crusoe (1966), teaches at Emory University.

ROGER B. LLOYD, D.D. (1901–1966), the late canon of Winchester Cathedral, wrote *The Borderland: An Exploration of Theology in English Literature* (1960).

KARL MARX (1818–1883), the German economist and political philosopher, wrote in *Das Kapital* (1867) the classical analysis of capitalist society.

JOHN ROBERT MOORE (1890–   ) is Distinguished Service Professor Emeritus at Indiana University. A leading Defoe scholar and editor, he is the author of *Daniel Defoe: Citizen of the Modern World* (1958), *A Checklist of the Writings of Daniel Defoe* (1960), and numerous other works.

MAXIMILLIAN E. NOVAK (1930–   ) is professor at the University of California at Los Angeles and author of *Economics and the Fiction of Daniel Defoe* (1962) and *Defoe and the Nature of Man* (1963). He is presently at work on a critical biography of Defoe.

GEORGE A. STARR (1934–   ), the author of *Defoe and Spiritual Autobiography* (1965), teaches at the University of California at Berkeley.

JAMES R. SUTHERLAND (1900–   ), Emeritus Professor of Modern English Literature at University College, London, is the author of more than a dozen books, including *Defoe* (1938), a biography, and *Background for Queen Anne* (1939).

E. M. W. TILLYARD (1889–1962), author of *The Epic Strain in the English Novel* (1958), was Master of Jesus College, Cambridge, and a distinguished scholar of Shakespeare and Milton. *The Elizabethan World Picture* (1943) is probably his best-known work.

IAN WATT (1917–   ), the author of *The Rise of the Novel* (1957), is now a professor at Leland Stanford University.

VIRGINIA WOOLF (1882–1941), the novelist and critic, wrote an earlier essay about Defoe in *The Common Reader* (1925) as well as the one reprinted above from *The Second Common Reader* (1932).

Selected Bibliography

Editions

The only definitive editions of *Robinson Crusoe* since 1719 are one published by the Shakespeare Head Press (Oxford: Basil Blackwell; Boston and New York: Houghton Mifflin Company, 1927–1928) and another edited by Henry C. Hutchins (New York: The Macmillan Company, 1930).

Commentaries

The reader interested in further study of *Robinson Crusoe* should consult first the works from which the Interpretations and View Points above were selected and then the works cited in the Introduction to this volume. The following additional works will also be helpful.

Andersen, Hans H., "The Paradox of Trade and Morality in Defoe," *Modern Philology*, XXXIX (1941), 23–46. (Discussion of the conflict between ethical values and commercialism in the early 18th century and of Defoe's resolution of it in his work.)

Ayres, Robert W., "Robinson Crusoe: 'Allusive Allegorick History'," *Publications of the Modern Language Association*, LXXXII (October 1967), 399–407. (Study of the *genre* of *Robinson Crusoe*).

Häusermann, Hans W., "Aspects of Life and Thought in *Robinson Crusoe*," *Review of English Studies*, XI (1935), 299–312, 439–56. (Study of the relative significance of the religious, commercial and politico-social aspects of life and thought in *Robinson Crusoe*.)

Hutchins, Henry L., *Robinson Crusoe and its Printing, 1719–1731* (New York: Columbia University Press, 1925).

Moffatt, James, "The Religion of Robinson Crusoe," *The Contemporary Review*, CXV (January–June 1919), 664–69. (Interesting early examination of the religious elements in *Robinson Crusoe*.)

Moore, John Robert, *A Checklist of the Writings of Daniel Defoe* (Bloomington: Indiana University Press, 1960).

Stamm, Rudolph G., "Daniel Defoe: An Artist in the Puritan Tradition," *Philological Quarterly*, XV (July 1936), 225–46. (Study of the influence of the moralistic and utilitarian Puritan aesthetic on Defoe's literary theory and practice.)

Professor Maximillian E. Novak is presently revising the list of Defoe's works for a new edition of the *Cambridge Bibliography of English Literature* and Professor William L. Payne, of the City University of New York, is preparing a list of works about Defoe.

TWENTIETH CENTURY
INTERPRETATIONS
MAYNARD MACK, *Series Editor*
Yale University

NOW AVAILABLE
Collections of Critical Essays
ON

ADVENTURES OF HUCKLEBERRY FINN
ALL FOR LOVE
THE AMBASSADORS
ARROWSMITH
AS YOU LIKE IT
BLEAK HOUSE
THE BOOK OF JOB
THE CASTLE
DOCTOR FAUSTUS
DUBLINERS
THE DUCHESS OF MALFI
EURIPIDES' ALCESTIS
THE FROGS
GRAY'S ELEGY
THE GREAT GATSBY
GULLIVER'S TRAVELS
HAMLET
HARD TIMES
HENRY IV, PART TWO
HENRY V
THE ICEMAN COMETH
JULIUS CAESAR
KEATS'S ODES
LORD JIM
MUCH ADO ABOUT NOTHING

OEDIPUS REX
THE OLD MAN AND THE SEA
PAMELA
PLAYBOY OF THE WESTERN WORLD
THE PORTRAIT OF A LADY
A PORTRAIT OF THE ARTIST AS A YOUNG MAN
PRIDE AND PREJUDICE
THE RIME OF THE ANCIENT MARINER
ROBINSON CRUSOE
SAMSON AGONISTES
THE SCARLET LETTER
SIR GAWAIN AND THE GREEN KNIGHT
THE SOUND AND THE FURY
THE TEMPEST
TOM JONES
TWELFTH NIGHT
UTOPIA
WALDEN
THE WASTE LAND
WUTHERING HEIGHTS